Praise for David Auburn's *Proof*

"David Auburn combines elements of mystery and surprise with old-fashioned storytelling to provide a compelling evening of theater . . . [*Proof* is a] smart and compassionate play of ideas."
　　　　　　　　　—David Kaufman, New York *Daily News*

"*Proof* surprises us with its aliveness . . . Mr. Auburn takes pleasure in knowledge . . . At the same time, he is unshowily fresh and humane, and he has written a lovely play."
　　　　　　　　　—John Heilpern, *The New York Observer*

"[A] wonderfully funny . . . ambitiously constructed work . . . Auburn's flair for the theatrical is a continual source of satisfaction."
　　　　　　　　　—Robert Hofler, *Variety*

"*Proof* demonstrates some beautiful and subtle insights about, and comparisons between, mathematical and real-life proof . . . A wonderful drama."
　　　　　　　　　—Daniel Rockmore, *The Chronicle of Higher Education*

"*Proof* is lively indeed . . . [It] bubbles with a chemistry of its own."
　　　　　　　　　—Amy Gamerman, *The Wall Street Journal*

David Auburn

Proof

David Auburn was born in Chicago, Illinois, and raised in Ohio and Arkansas. He has received a Guggenheim Fellowship and, for *Proof*, the Kesselring Prize. He lives in Brooklyn, New York.

proof

proof

A play by **DAVID AUBURN**

FARRAR, STRAUS AND GIROUX

NEW YORK

Farrar, Straus and Giroux
18 West 18th Street, New York 10011

Library of Congress Cataloging-in-Publication Data
Auburn, David, 1969–
    Proof : a play / by David Auburn.— 1st ed.
        p. cm.
    Includes bibliographical references and index.
    ISBN: 978-0-571-19997-6 (pbk. : alk. paper)
    1. Man-woman relationships—Drama. 2. Fathers—Death—Drama.
    3. Mathematicians—Drama. I. Title.

    PS3551.U28 P7 2001
    812'.6—dc21

                                                00050284

Designed by Jessica Shatan

www.fsgbooks.com

37   36   35   34   33   32   31

In memory of Benjamin Auburn (1972–2000)

proof

Originally produced by the Manhattan Theatre Club on May 23, 2000. Subsequently produced on Broadway by the Manhattan Theatre Club, Lynne Meadow, artistic director; Barry Grove, executive producer; Roger Berlind, Carole Shorenstein Hays, Jujamcyn Theatres, Ostar Enterprises, Daryl Roth, and Stuart Thompson on October 24, 2000.

Proof was directed by Daniel Sullivan; sets were designed by John Lee Beatty; costumes by Jess Goldstein; lights by Pat Collins; and sound by John Gromada. The production stage manager was James Harker.

CAST OF CHARACTERS
Robert   Larry Bryggman
Catherine   Mary-Louise Parker
Hal   Ben Shenkman
Claire   Johanna Day

SETTING
The back porch of a house in Chicago

CHARACTERS
Robert, fifties
Catherine, twenty-five
Hal, twenty-eight
Claire, twenty-nine

Act One

Scene 1

Night. CATHERINE *sits in a chair. She is exhausted, haphazardly dressed. Eyes closed.* ROBERT *is standing behind her. He is* CATHERINE's *father. Rumpled academic look.* CATHERINE *does not know he is there. After a moment:*

ROBERT: Can't sleep?

CATHERINE: Jesus, you scared me.

ROBERT: Sorry.

CATHERINE: What are you doing here?

ROBERT: I thought I'd check up on you. Why aren't you in bed?

CATHERINE: Your student is still here. He's up in your study.

ROBERT: He can let himself out.

CATHERINE: I might as well wait up till he's done.

ROBERT: He's not my student anymore. He's teaching now. Bright kid.

(Beat.)

CATHERINE: What time is it?

ROBERT: It's almost one.

CATHERINE: Huh.

ROBERT: After midnight . . .

CATHERINE: So?

ROBERT: So: *(He indicates something on the table behind him: a bottle of champagne.)* Happy birthday.

CATHERINE: Dad.

ROBERT: Do I ever forget?

CATHERINE: Thank you.

ROBERT: Twenty-five. I can't believe it.

CATHERINE: Neither can I. Should we have it now?

ROBERT: It's up to you.

CATHERINE: Yes.

ROBERT: You want me to open it?

CATHERINE: Let me. Last time you opened a bottle of champagne out here you broke a window.

ROBERT: That was a long time ago. I resent your bringing it up.

CATHERINE: You're lucky you didn't lose an eye.

(Pop. The bottle foams.)

ROBERT: Twenty-five!

CATHERINE: I feel old.

ROBERT: You're a kid.

CATHERINE: Glasses?

ROBERT: Goddamn it, I forgot the glasses. Do you want me to—

CATHERINE: Nah.

*(*CATHERINE *drinks from the bottle. A long pull.* ROBERT *watches her.)*

ROBERT: I hope you like it. I wasn't sure what to get you.

CATHERINE: This is the worst champagne I have ever tasted.

ROBERT: I am proud to say I don't know anything about wines. I hate those kind of people who are always talking about "vintages."

CATHERINE: It's not even champagne.

ROBERT: The bottle was the right shape.

CATHERINE: "Great Lakes Vineyards." I didn't know they made wine in Wisconsin.

ROBERT: A girl who's drinking from the bottle shouldn't complain. Don't guzzle it. It's an elegant beverage. Sip.

CATHERINE: *(Offering the bottle)* Do you—

ROBERT: No, go ahead.

CATHERINE: You sure?

ROBERT: Yeah. It's your birthday.

CATHERINE: Happy birthday to me.

ROBERT: What are you going to do on your birthday?

CATHERINE: Drink this. Have some.

ROBERT: No. I hope you're not spending your birthday alone.

CATHERINE: I'm not alone.

ROBERT: I don't count.

CATHERINE: Why not?

ROBERT: I'm your old man. Go out with some friends.

CATHERINE: Right.

ROBERT: Your friends aren't taking you out?

CATHERINE: No.

ROBERT: Why not?

CATHERINE: Because in order for your friends to take you out you generally have to have friends.

ROBERT: *(Dismissive)* Oh—

CATHERINE: It's funny how that works.

ROBERT: You have friends. What about that cute blonde, what was her name?

CATHERINE: What?

ROBERT: She lives over on Ellis Avenue—you used to spend every minute together.

CATHERINE: Cindy Jacobsen?

ROBERT: Cindy Jacobsen!

CATHERINE: That was in *third grade*, Dad. Her family moved to Florida in 1983.

ROBERT: What about Claire?

CATHERINE: She's not my friend, she's my sister. And she's in New York. And I don't like her.

ROBERT: I thought she was coming in.

CATHERINE: Not till tomorrow.

(Beat.)

ROBERT: My advice, if you find yourself awake late at night, is to sit down and do some mathematics.

CATHERINE: Oh please.

ROBERT: We could do some together.

CATHERINE: No.

ROBERT: Why not?

CATHERINE: I can't think of anything worse. You sure you don't want any?

ROBERT: Yeah, thanks. You used to love it.

CATHERINE: Not anymore.

ROBERT: You knew what a prime number was before you could read.

CATHERINE: Well now I've forgotten.

ROBERT: *(Hard)* Don't waste your talent, Catherine.

(Beat.)

CATHERINE: I knew you'd say something like that.

ROBERT: I realize you've had a difficult time.

CATHERINE: Thanks.

ROBERT: That's not an excuse. Don't be lazy.

CATHERINE: I haven't been lazy, I've been taking care of you.

ROBERT: Kid, I've seen you. You sleep till noon, you eat junk, you don't work, the dishes pile up in the sink. If you go out it's to buy magazines. You come back with a stack of magazines this high— I don't know how you read that crap. And those are the good days. Some days you don't get up, you don't get out of bed.

CATHERINE: Those are the good days.

ROBERT: Bullshit. Those days are lost. You threw them away. And you'll never know what else you threw away with them—the work you lost, the ideas you didn't have, discoveries you never made because you were moping in your bed at four in the afternoon. *(Beat.)* You know I'm right. *(Beat.)*

CATHERINE: I've lost a few days.

ROBERT: How many?

CATHERINE: Oh, I don't know.

ROBERT: I bet you do.

CATHERINE: What?

ROBERT: I bet you count.

CATHERINE: Knock it off.

ROBERT: Well do you know or don't you?

CATHERINE: I don't.

ROBERT: Of course you do. How many days have you lost?

CATHERINE: A month. Around a month.

ROBERT: Exactly.

CATHERINE: Goddamn it, I don't—

ROBERT: *How many?*

CATHERINE: Thirty-three days.

ROBERT: Exactly?

CATHERINE: I don't know.

ROBERT: Be precise, for Chrissake.

CATHERINE: I slept till noon today.

ROBERT: Call it thirty-three and a quarter days.

CATHERINE: Yes, all right.

ROBERT: You're kidding!

CATHERINE: No.

ROBERT: Amazing number!

CATHERINE: It's a depressing fucking number.

ROBERT: Catherine, if every day you say you've lost were a year, it would be a very interesting fucking number.

CATHERINE: Thirty-three and a quarter years is not interesting.

ROBERT: Stop it. You know exactly what I mean.

CATHERINE: *(Conceding)* 1729 weeks.

ROBERT: 1729. Great number. The smallest number express-ible—

CATHERINE: —expressible as the sum of two cubes in two different ways.

ROBERT: 12 cubed plus 1 cubed equals 1729.

CATHERINE: And 10 cubed plus 9 cubed. Yes, we've got it, thank you.

ROBERT: You see? Even your depression is mathematical. Stop moping and get to work. The kind of potential you have—

CATHERINE: I haven't done anything good.

ROBERT: You're young. You've got time.

CATHERINE: I do?

ROBERT: *Yes.*

CATHERINE: By the time you were my age you were famous.

ROBERT: By the time I was your age I'd already done my best work.

(Beat.)

CATHERINE: What about after?

ROBERT: After what?

CATHERINE: After you got sick.

ROBERT: What about it?

CATHERINE: You couldn't work then.

ROBERT: No, if anything I was sharper.

CATHERINE: *(She can't help it: she laughs.)* Dad.

ROBERT: I was. Hey, it's true. The clarity—that was the amazing thing. No doubts.

CATHERINE: You were happy?

ROBERT: Yeah, I was busy.

CATHERINE: Not the same thing.

ROBERT: I don't see the difference. I knew what I wanted to do and I did it.

If I wanted to work a problem all day long, I did it.

If I wanted to look for information—secrets, complex and tantalizing messages—I could find them all around me. In the air. In a pile of fallen leaves some neighbor raked together. In box scores in the paper, written in the steam coming up off a cup of coffee. The whole world was talking to me.

If I just wanted to close my eyes, sit quietly on the porch and listen for the messages, I did that.

It was wonderful.

(Beat.)

CATHERINE: How old were you? When it started.

ROBERT: Mid-twenties. Twenty-three, four. *(Beat.)* Is that what you're worried about?

CATHERINE: I've thought about it.

ROBERT: Just getting a year older means nothing, Catherine.

CATHERINE: It's not just getting older.

ROBERT: It's me.

(Beat.)

CATHERINE: I've thought about it.

ROBERT: Really?

CATHERINE: How could I not?

ROBERT: Well if that's why you're worried you're not keeping up with the medical literature. There are all kinds of factors. It's not simply something you inherit. Just because I went bughouse doesn't mean you will.

CATHERINE: Dad . . .

ROBERT: Listen to me. Life changes fast in your early twenties and it shakes you up. You're feeling down. It's been a bad week. You've had a lousy couple years, no one knows that better than me. But you're gonna be okay.

CATHERINE: Yeah?

ROBERT: Yes. I promise you. Push yourself. Don't read so many magazines. Sit down and get the machinery going and I swear to God you'll feel fine. The simple fact that we can talk about this together is a good sign.

CATHERINE: A good sign?

ROBERT: Yes!

CATHERINE: How could it be a good sign?

ROBERT: Because! Crazy people don't sit around wondering if they're nuts.

CATHERINE: They don't?

ROBERT: Of course not. They've got better things to do. Take it from me. A very good sign that you're crazy is an inability to ask the question "Am I crazy?"

CATHERINE: Even if the answer is yes?

ROBERT: Crazy people don't ask. You see?

CATHERINE: Yes.

ROBERT: So if you're asking . . .

CATHERINE: I'm not.

ROBERT: But if you were, it would be a very good sign.

CATHERINE: A good sign . . .

ROBERT: A good sign that you're fine.

CATHERINE: Right.

ROBERT: You see? You've just gotta think these things through. Now come on, what do you say? Let's call it a night; you go up, get some sleep, and then in the morning you can—

CATHERINE: Wait. No.

ROBERT: What's the matter?

CATHERINE: It doesn't work.

ROBERT: Why not?

CATHERINE: It doesn't make sense.

ROBERT: Sure it does.

CATHERINE: No.

ROBERT: Where's the problem?

CATHERINE: The problem is you are crazy!

ROBERT: What difference does that make?

CATHERINE: You admitted— You just told me that you are.

ROBERT: So?

CATHERINE: You said a crazy person would never admit that.

ROBERT: Yeah, but it's . . . Oh. I see.

CATHERINE: So?

ROBERT: It's a point.

CATHERINE: So how can you admit it?

ROBERT: Well. Because I'm also dead. *(Beat.)* Aren't I?

CATHERINE: You died a week ago.

ROBERT: Heart failure. Quick. The funeral's tomorrow.

CATHERINE: That's why Claire's flying in from New York.

ROBERT: Yes.

CATHERINE: You're sitting here. You're giving me advice. You brought me champagne.

ROBERT: Yes.

(Beat.)

CATHERINE: Which means . . .

ROBERT: For you?

CATHERINE: Yes.

ROBERT: For you, Catherine, my daughter, who I love very much . . .
    It could be a bad sign.

(They sit together for a moment. Noise off. HAL *enters, semi-hip clothes. He carries a backpack and a jacket, folded. He lets the door go and it bangs shut.* CATHERINE *sits up with a jolt.)*

CATHERINE: What?

HAL: Oh God, sorry—did I wake you?

CATHERINE: What?

HAL: Were you asleep?

(Beat. ROBERT *is gone.)*

CATHERINE: You scared me, for Chrissake. What are you doing?

HAL: I'm sorry. I didn't realize it had gotten so late. I'm done for the night.

CATHERINE: Good.

HAL: Drinking alone?

*(*CATHERINE *realizes she is holding the champagne bottle. She puts it down quickly.)*

CATHERINE: Yes.

HAL: Champagne, huh?

CATHERINE: Yes.

HAL: Celebrating?

CATHERINE: No. I just like champagne.

HAL: It's festive.

CATHERINE: What?

HAL: *Festive. (He makes an awkward "party" gesture.)*

CATHERINE: Do you want some?

HAL: Sure.

CATHERINE: *(Gives him the bottle.)* I'm done. You can take the rest with you.

HAL: Oh. No thanks.

CATHERINE: Take it, I'm done.

HAL: No, I shouldn't. I'm driving. *(Beat.)* Well I can let myself out.

CATHERINE: Good.

HAL: When should I come back?

CATHERINE: Come back?

HAL: Yeah. I'm nowhere near finished. Maybe tomorrow?

CATHERINE: We have a funeral tomorrow.

HAL: God, you're right, I'm sorry. I was going to attend, if that's all right.

CATHERINE: Yes.

HAL: What about Sunday? Will you be around?

CATHERINE: You've had three days.

HAL: I'd love to get in some more time up there.

CATHERINE: How much longer do you need?

HAL: Another week. At least.

CATHERINE: Are you joking?

HAL: No. Do you know how much stuff there is?

CATHERINE: A week?

HAL: I know you don't need anybody in your hair right now. Look, I spent the last couple days getting everything sorted out. It's mostly notebooks. He dated them all; now that I've got them in order I don't have to work here. I could take some stuff home, read it, bring it back.

CATHERINE: No.

HAL: I'll be careful.

CATHERINE: My father wouldn't want anything moved and I don't want anything to leave this house.

HAL: Then I should work here. I'll stay out of the way.

CATHERINE: You're wasting your time.

HAL: Someone needs to go through your dad's papers.

CATHERINE: There's nothing up there. It's garbage.

HAL: There are a hundred and three notebooks.

CATHERINE: I've looked at those. It's gibberish.

HAL: Someone should read them.

CATHERINE: He was crazy.

HAL: Yes, but he wrote them.

CATHERINE: He was a graphomaniac, Harold. Do you know what that is?

HAL: I know. He wrote compulsively. Call me Hal.

CATHERINE: There's no connection between the ideas. There's no ideas. It's like a monkey at a typewriter. A hundred and three notebooks full of bullshit.

HAL: Let's make sure they're bullshit.

CATHERINE: I'm sure.

HAL: I'm prepared to look at every page. Are you?

CATHERINE: No. *I'm* not crazy.

(*Beat.*)

HAL: Well, I'm gonna be late . . . Some friends of mine are in this band. They're playing at a bar up on Diversey. Way down the bill, they're probably going on around two, two-thirty. I said I'd be there.

CATHERINE: Great.

HAL: They're all in the math department. They're really good.

They have this great song—you'd like it—called "i"—
lower-case I. They just stand there and don't play anything
for three minutes.

CATHERINE: "Imaginary Number."

HAL: It's a math joke. You see why they're way down the bill.

CATHERINE: Long drive to see some nerds in a band.

HAL: God I hate when people say that. It is not that long a
drive.

CATHERINE: So they are nerds.

HAL: Oh they're raging geeks. But they're geeks who, you
know, can dress themselves . . . hold down a job at a major
university . . . Some of them have switched from glasses to
contacts. They play sports, they play in a band, they get laid
surprisingly often, so in that sense they sort of make you
question the whole set of terms: geek, nerd, wonk, dweeb,
dilbert, paste-eater.

CATHERINE: You're in this band, aren't you?

HAL: Okay, yes. I play drums. You want to come? I never sing,
I swear to God.

CATHERINE: No thanks.

HAL: All right. Look, Catherine, Monday: what do you say?

CATHERINE: Don't you have a job?

HAL: Yeah, I have a full teaching load this quarter plus my own
work.

CATHERINE: Plus band practice.

HAL: I don't have time to do this but I'm going to. If you'll let
me. *(Beat.)* I loved your dad. I don't believe a mind like his
can just shut down. He had lucid moments. He had a lucid
year, a whole year four years ago.

CATHERINE: It wasn't a year. It was more like nine months.

HAL: A school year. He was advising students . . . I was stalled on
my Ph.D. I was this close to quitting. I met with your dad
and he put me on the right track with my research. I owe him.

CATHERINE: Sorry.

HAL: Look. Let me— You're twenty-five, right?

CATHERINE: How old are you?

HAL: It doesn't matter. Listen.

CATHERINE: Fuck you, how old are you?

HAL: I'm twenty-eight, all right? When your dad was younger than both of us, he made major contributions to three fields: game theory, algebraic geometry, and nonlinear operator theory. Most of us never get our heads around one. He basically invented the mathematical techniques for studying rational behavior, and he gave the astrophysicists plenty to work over too. Okay?

CATHERINE: Don't lecture me.

HAL: I'm not. I'm telling you, if I came up with one-tenth of the shit your dad produced, I could write my own ticket to any math department in the country.

(Beat.)

CATHERINE: Give me your backpack.

HAL: What?

CATHERINE: Give me your backpack.

HAL: Why?

CATHERINE: I want to look inside it.

HAL: What?

CATHERINE: Open it and give it to me.

HAL: Oh come on.

CATHERINE: You're not taking anything out of this house.

HAL: I wouldn't do that.

CATHERINE: You're hoping to find something upstairs that you can publish.

HAL: Sure.

CATHERINE: Then you can write your own ticket.

HAL: What? No! It would be under your dad's name. It would be for your dad.

CATHERINE: I don't believe you. You have a notebook in that backpack.

HAL: What are you talking about?

CATHERINE: Give it to me.

HAL: You're being a little bit paranoid.

CATHERINE: *Paranoid?*

HAL: Maybe a little.

CATHERINE: Fuck you, *Hal. I know* you have one of my notebooks.

HAL: I think you should calm down and think about what you're saying.

CATHERINE: I'm saying you're lying to me and stealing my family's property.

HAL: And I think that sounds paranoid.

CATHERINE: Just because I'm paranoid doesn't mean there isn't something in that backpack.

HAL: *You just said yourself there's nothing up there.* Didn't you?

CATHERINE: I—

HAL: Didn't you say that?

CATHERINE: Yes.

HAL: So what would I take? Right?

(Beat.)

CATHERINE: You're right.

HAL: Thank you.

CATHERINE: So you don't need to come back.

HAL: *(Sighs.)* Please. Someone should know for sure whether—

CATHERINE: *I lived with him.*

I spent my life with him. I fed him. Talked to him. Tried to listen when he talked. Talked to people who weren't there . . . Watched him shuffling around like a ghost. A very smelly ghost. He was filthy. I had to make sure he bathed. My own father.

HAL: I'm sorry. I shouldn't have . . .

CATHERINE: After my mother died it was just me here. I tried to keep him happy no matter what idiotic project he was doing. He used to read all day. He kept demanding more and more books. I took them out of the library by the carload. We had hundreds upstairs. Then I realized he wasn't reading: he believed aliens were sending him messages through the Dewey decimal numbers on the library books. He was trying to work out the code.

HAL: What kind of messages?

CATHERINE: Beautiful mathematics. The most elegant proofs, perfect proofs, proofs like music.

HAL: Sounds good.

CATHERINE: Plus fashion tips, knock-knock jokes—I mean it was *nuts*, okay?

HAL: He was ill. It was a tragedy.

CATHERINE: Later the writing phase: scribbling nineteen, twenty hours a day . . . I ordered him a case of notebooks and he used every one.

I dropped out of school . . .

I'm glad he's dead.

HAL: I understand why you'd feel that way.

CATHERINE: Fuck you.

HAL: You're right. I can't imagine dealing with that. It must have been awful. I know you—

CATHERINE: You don't know me. I want to be alone. I don't want him around.

HAL: *(Confused)* Him? I don't—

CATHERINE: You. I don't want you here.

HAL: Why?

CATHERINE: He's dead.

HAL: But I'm not—

CATHERINE: *He's* dead; I don't need any *protégés* around.

HAL: There will be others.

CATHERINE: What?

HAL: You think I'm the only one? People are already working over his stuff. Someone's gonna read those notebooks.

CATHERINE: I'll do it.

HAL: No, you—

CATHERINE: He's my father, I'll do it.

HAL: You can't.

CATHERINE: Why not?

HAL: You don't have the math. It's all just squiggles on a page. You wouldn't know the good stuff from the junk.

CATHERINE: It's all junk.

HAL: If it's not we can't afford to miss any through carelessness.

CATHERINE: I know mathematics.

HAL: If there was anything up there it would be pretty high-order. It would take a professional to recognize it.

CATHERINE: I think I could recognize it.

HAL: *(Patient)* Cathy . . .

CATHERINE: *What?*

HAL: I know your dad taught you some basic stuff, but come on.

CATHERINE: You don't think I could do it.

HAL: I'm sorry: I know that you couldn't. *(Beat.* CATHERINE *snatches his backpack.)* Hey! Oh come on. Give me a break. *(*CATHERINE *opens the backpack and rifles through it.)* This isn't an airport.

*(*CATHERINE *removes items one by one. A water bottle. Some workout clothes. An orange. Drumsticks. Nothing else. She puts everything back in and gives it back. Beat.)*

CATHERINE: You can come tomorrow.

(Beat. They are both embarrassed.)

HAL: The university health service is uh very good.

My mom died a couple years ago and I was pretty broken up. Also my work wasn't going that well . . . I went over and talked to this doctor. I saw her for a couple months and it really helped.

CATHERINE: I'm fine.

(Beat.)

HAL: Also exercise is great. I run along the lake a couple of mornings a week. It's not too cold yet. If you wanted to come sometime I could pick you up. We wouldn't have to talk . . .

CATHERINE: No thanks.

HAL: All right. I'm gonna be late for the show. I better go.

CATHERINE: Okay.

(Beat.)

HAL: It's seriously like twenty minutes up to the club. We go on, we play, we're terrible but we buy everyone drinks afterward to make up for it. You're home by four, four-thirty, tops . . .

CATHERINE: Good night.

HAL: Good night. (He starts to exit. He has forgotten his jacket.)

CATHERINE: Wait, your coat.

HAL: No, you don't have to—

(CATHERINE picks up his jacket. As she does, a composition book that was folded up in the coat falls to the floor. Beat. She picks it up, trembling with rage.)

CATHERINE: I'm paranoid?

HAL: Wait.

CATHERINE: You think I should go jogging?

HAL: Just hold on.

CATHERINE: Get out!

HAL: Can I please just—

CATHERINE: Get the fuck out of my house.

HAL: Listen to me for a minute.

CATHERINE: (Waving the book) You stole this!

HAL: Let me explain!

CATHERINE: You stole it from me, you stole it from my father—

(HAL snatches the book.)

HAL: I want to show you something. Will you calm down?

CATHERINE: Give it back.

HAL: Just wait a minute.

CATHERINE: I'm calling the police. *(She picks up the phone and dials.)*

HAL: Don't. Look, I borrowed the book, all right? I'm sorry, I just picked it up before I came downstairs and thought I'd—

CATHERINE: *(On phone)* Hello?

HAL: I did it for a reason.

CATHERINE: Hello, police? I— Yes, I'd like to report a robbery in progress.

HAL: I noticed something—something your father wrote. All right? Not math, something he *wrote*. Here, let me show you.

CATHERINE: *A robbery.*

HAL: Will you put the fucking phone down and listen to me?

CATHERINE: *(On phone)* Yes, I'm at 5724 South—

HAL: It's about you. See? *You.* It was written about you. Here's your name: *Cathy.* See?

CATHERINE: South . . .

(CATHERINE pauses. She seems to be listening. HAL reads.)

HAL: "A good day. Some very good news from Catherine." I didn't know what that referred to, but I thought you might . . .

CATHERINE: When did he write this?

HAL: I think four years ago. The handwriting is steady. It must have been during his remission. There's more. *(A moment. CATHERINE hangs up the phone.)* "Machinery not working yet but I am patient." "The machinery" is what he called his mind, his ability to do mathematics.

CATHERINE: I know.

HAL: *(Reads)* "I know I'll get there. I am an auto mechanic who after years of greasy work on a hopeless wreck turns the ignition and hears a faint cough. I am not driving yet, but there's cause for optimism. Talking with students helps. So does being outside, eating meals in restaurants, riding buses, all the activities of 'normal' life.

"Most of all Cathy. The years she has lost caring for me. I almost wrote 'wasted.' Yet her refusal to let me be institutionalized—her keeping me at home, caring for me herself, has certainly saved my life. Made writing this possible. Made it possible to imagine doing math again. Where does her strength come from? I can never repay her.

"Today is her birthday: she is twenty-one. I'm taking her to dinner." Dated September 4. That's tomorrow.

CATHERINE: It's today.

HAL: You're right. *(He gives her the book.)* I thought you might want to see it. I shouldn't have tried to sneak it out. Tomorrow I was going to—it sounds stupid now. I was going to wrap it. Happy birthday.

(HAL exits. CATHERINE is alone. She puts her head in her hands. She weeps. Eventually she stops, wipes her eyes. From off: a police siren, drawing closer.)

CATHERINE: Shit.

fade

Scene 2

The next morning. CLAIRE, *stylish, attractive, drinks coffee from a mug. She has brought bagels and fruit on a tray out to the porch. She arranges them on two plates. She notices the champagne bottle lying on the floor. She picks it up and sets it on a table.* CATHERINE *enters. Her hair is wet from a shower.*

CLAIRE: Better. Much.

CATHERINE: Thanks.

CLAIRE: Feel better?

CATHERINE: Yeah.

CLAIRE: You look a million times better. Have some coffee.

CATHERINE: Okay.

CLAIRE: How do you take it?

CATHERINE: Black.

CLAIRE: Have a little milk. *(She pours.)* Want a banana? It's a good thing I brought food: there was nothing in the house.

CATHERINE: I've been meaning to go shopping.

CLAIRE: Have a bagel.

CATHERINE: No. I hate breakfast. *(Beat.)*

CLAIRE: You didn't put on the dress.

CATHERINE: Didn't really feel like it.

CLAIRE: Don't you want to try it on? See if it fits?

CATHERINE: I'll put it on later.

(Beat.)

CLAIRE: If you want to dry your hair I have a hair dryer.

CATHERINE: Nah.

CLAIRE: Did you use that conditioner I brought you?

CATHERINE: No, shit, I forgot.

CLAIRE: It's my favorite. You'll love it, Katie. I want you to try it.

CATHERINE: I'll use it next time.

CLAIRE: You'll like it. It has jojoba.

CATHERINE: What is "jojoba"?

CLAIRE: It's something they put in for healthy hair.

CATHERINE: Hair is dead.

CLAIRE: What?

CATHERINE: It's dead tissue. You can't make it "healthy."

CLAIRE: Whatever, it's something that's good for your hair.

CATHERINE: What, a chemical?

CLAIRE: No, it's organic.

CATHERINE: Well it can be organic and still be a chemical.

CLAIRE: I don't know what it is.

CATHERINE: Haven't you ever heard of organic chemistry?

CLAIRE: It makes my hair feel, look, and smell good. That's the extent of my information about it. You might like it if you decide to use it.

CATHERINE: Thanks, I'll try it.

CLAIRE: Good. *(Beat.)* If the dress doesn't fit we can go downtown and exchange it.

CATHERINE: Okay.

CLAIRE: I'll take you to lunch.

CATHERINE: Great.

CLAIRE: Maybe Sunday before I go back. Do you need anything?

CATHERINE: Like clothes?

CLAIRE: Or anything. While I'm here.

CATHERINE: Nah, I'm cool.

(Beat.)

CLAIRE: I thought we'd have some people over tonight. If you're feeling okay.

CATHERINE: I'm feeling okay, Claire, stop saying that.

CLAIRE: You don't have any plans?

CATHERINE: No.

CLAIRE: I ordered some food. Wine, beer.

CATHERINE: We are burying Dad this afternoon.

CLAIRE: I think it will be all right. Anyone who's been to the funeral and wants to come over for something to eat can. And it's the only time I can see any old Chicago friends. It'll be nice. It's a funeral but we don't have to be completely grim about it. *If* it's okay with you.

CATHERINE: Yes, sure.

CLAIRE: It's been a stressful time. It would be good to relax in a low-key way.

Mitch says Hi.

CATHERINE: Hi Mitch.

CLAIRE: He's really sorry he couldn't come.

CATHERINE: Yeah, he's gonna miss all the fun.

CLAIRE: He wanted to see you. He sends his love. I told him you'd see him soon enough. *(Beat.)* We're getting married.

CATHERINE: No shit.

CLAIRE: Yes! We just decided.

CATHERINE: Yikes.

CLAIRE: Yes!

CATHERINE: When?

CLAIRE: January.

CATHERINE: Huh.

CLAIRE: We're not going to do a huge thing. His folks are gone too. Just City Hall, then a big dinner at our favorite restaurant for all our friends. And you, of course. I hope you'll be in the wedding.

CATHERINE: Yeah. Of course. Congratulations, Claire, I'm really happy for you.

CLAIRE: Thanks. Me too. We just decided it was time. His job is great. I just got promoted . . .

CATHERINE: Huh.

CLAIRE: You will come?

CATHERINE: Yes, sure. January? I mean, I don't have to check my calendar or anything. Sure.

CLAIRE: That makes me very happy. *(Beat. From here on* CLAIRE *treads gingerly.)*

CLAIRE: How are you?

CATHERINE: Okay.

CLAIRE: How are you feeling about everything?

CATHERINE: About "everything"?

CLAIRE: About Dad.

CATHERINE: What about him?

CLAIRE: How are you feeling about his death? Are you all right?

CATHERINE: Yes, I am.

CLAIRE: Honestly?

CATHERINE: Yes.

CLAIRE: I think in some ways it was the "right time." If there is ever a right time.

Do you know what you want to do now?

CATHERINE: No.

CLAIRE: Do you want to stay here?

CATHERINE: I don't know.

CLAIRE: Do you want to go back to school?

CATHERINE: I haven't thought about it.

CLAIRE: Well there's a lot to think about.

How do you feel?

CATHERINE: Physically? Great. Except my hair seems kind of unhealthy, I wish there were something I could do about that.

CLAIRE: Come on, Catherine.

CATHERINE: What is the point of all these questions?

(Beat.)

CLAIRE: Katie, some policemen came by while you were in the shower.

CATHERINE: Yeah?

CLAIRE: They said they were "checking up" on things here. Seeing how everything was this morning.

CATHERINE: *(Neutral)* That was nice.

CLAIRE: They told me they responded to a call last night and came to the house.

CATHERINE: Yeah?

CLAIRE: Did you call the police last night?

CATHERINE: Yeah.

CLAIRE: Why?

CATHERINE: I thought the house was being robbed.

CLAIRE: But it wasn't.

CATHERINE: No. I changed my mind.

(Beat.)

CLAIRE: First you call 911 with an emergency and then you hang up on them—

CATHERINE: I didn't really want them to come.

CLAIRE: So why did you call?

CATHERINE: I was trying to get this guy out of the house.

CLAIRE: Who?

CATHERINE: One of Dad's students.

CLAIRE: Dad hasn't had any students for years.

CATHERINE: No, he *was* Dad's student. Now he's—he's a mathematician.

CLAIRE: Why was he in the house in the first place?

CATHERINE: Well he's been coming here to look at Dad's notebooks.

CLAIRE: In the middle of the night?

CATHERINE: It was late. I was waiting for him to finish, and last night I thought he might have been stealing them.

CLAIRE: Stealing the notebooks.

CATHERINE: *Yes.* So I told him to go.

CLAIRE: Was he stealing them?

CATHERINE: Yes. That's why I called the police—

CLAIRE: What is this man's name?

CATHERINE: Hal. Harold. Harold Dobbs.

CLAIRE: The police said you were the only one here.

CATHERINE: He left before they got here.

CLAIRE: With the notebooks?

CATHERINE: No, Claire, don't be stupid, there are over a hundred notebooks. He was only stealing *one*, but he was stealing it so he could give it *back* to me, so I let him go so he could play with his band on the north side.

CLAIRE: His band?

CATHERINE: He was late. He wanted me to come with him but I was like, Yeah, right.

(Beat.)

CLAIRE: *(Gently)* Is "Harold Dobbs" your boyfriend?

CATHERINE: No!

CLAIRE: Are you sleeping with him?

CATHERINE: What? Euughh! No! He's a math geek!

CLAIRE: And he's in a band? A rock band?

CATHERINE: No, a marching band. He plays trombone. Yes, a rock band!

CLAIRE: What is the name of his band?

CATHERINE: How should I know?

CLAIRE: "Harold Dobbs" didn't tell you the name of his rock band?

CATHERINE: No. I don't know. Look in the paper. They were playing last night. They do a song called "Imaginary Number" that doesn't exist.

(Beat.)

CLAIRE: I'm sorry, I'm just trying to understand: is "Harold Dobbs"—

CATHERINE: Stop saying "Harold Dobbs."

CLAIRE: Is this . . . person . . .

CATHERINE: *Harold Dobbs exists.*

CLAIRE: I'm sure he does.

CATHERINE: He's a mathematician at the University of Chicago. Call the fucking math department.

CLAIRE: Don't get upset. I'm just trying to understand! I mean if you found out some creepy grad student was trying to take some of Dad's papers and you called the police, I'd understand, and if you were out here partying, drinking with your boyfriend, I'd understand. But the two stories don't go together.

CATHERINE: Because you made up the "boyfriend" story. I was here *alone.*

CLAIRE: Harold Dobbs wasn't here?

CATHERINE: No, he— *Yes*, he was here, but we weren't partying!

CLAIRE: You weren't drinking with him?

CATHERINE: No!

CLAIRE: *(She holds up the champagne bottle.)* This was sitting right here. Who were you drinking champagne with?

(CATHERINE hesitates.)

CATHERINE: With no one.

CLAIRE: Are you sure?

CATHERINE: Yes.

(Beat.)

CLAIRE: The police said you were abusive. *(CATHERINE doesn't say anything.)* They said you're lucky they didn't haul you in.

CATHERINE: These guys were assholes, Claire. They wouldn't go away. They wanted me to fill out a report . . .

CLAIRE: Were you abusive?

CATHERINE: This one cop kept spitting on me when he talked. It was disgusting.

CLAIRE: Did you use the word "dickhead"?

CATHERINE: Oh I don't remember.

CLAIRE: Did you tell one cop . . . to go fuck the other cop's mother?

CATHERINE: *No.*

CLAIRE: That's what they said.

CATHERINE: Not with that phrasing.

CLAIRE: Did you strike one of them?

CATHERINE: They were trying to come in the house!

CLAIRE: Oh my God.

CATHERINE: I might have *pushed* him a little.

CLAIRE: They said you were either drunk or disturbed.

CATHERINE: They wanted to come in here and *search my house—*

CLAIRE: *You* called *them.*

CATHERINE: Yes but I didn't actually *want* them to come. But they did come and then they started acting like they owned the place, pushing me around, calling me "girly," smirking at me, laughing: they were assholes.

CLAIRE: These guys seemed perfectly nice. They were off-duty and they took the trouble to come back here at the end of their shift to check up on you. They were very polite.

CATHERINE: Well people are nicer to you.

(Beat.)

CLAIRE: Katie. Would you like to come to New York?

CATHERINE: Yes, I told you, I'll come in January.

CLAIRE: You could come sooner. We'd love to have you. You could stay with us. It'd be fun.

CATHERINE: I don't want to.

CLAIRE: Mitch has become an *excellent* cook. It's like his hobby now. He buys all these gadgets. Garlic press, olive oil sprayer . . . Every night there's something new. Delicious, wonderful meals. The other day he made vegetarian chili!

CATHERINE: What the fuck are you talking about?

CLAIRE: Stay with us for a while. We would have so much fun.

CATHERINE: Thanks, I'm okay here.

CLAIRE: Chicago is dead. New York is so much more fun, you can't believe it.

CATHERINE: The "fun" thing is really not where my focus is at the moment.

CLAIRE: I think New York would be a really fun and . . . safe . . . place for you to—

CATHERINE: I don't need a safe place and I don't want to have any fun! I'm perfectly fine here.

CLAIRE: You look tired. I think you could use some downtime.

CATHERINE: Downtime?

CLAIRE: Katie, please. You've had a very hard time.

CATHERINE: I'm *perfectly okay*.

CLAIRE: I think you're upset and exhausted.

CATHERINE: I was *fine* till you got here.

CLAIRE: Yes, but you—

HAL: *(From off)* Catherine?

CLAIRE: Who is that?

(Beat. HAL *enters.)*

HAL: Hey, I—

*(*CATHERINE *stands and points triumphantly at him.)*

CATHERINE: *Harold Dobbs!*

HAL: *(Confused)* Hi.

CATHERINE: *Okay?* I really don't need this, Claire. I'm fine, you know, I'm totally fine, and then you swoop in here with these questions, and "Are you okay?" and your soothing tone of voice and "Oh, the poor policemen"—I think the police can handle themselves!—and bagels and bananas and jojoba and "Come to New York" and vegetarian *chili.* I mean it really pisses me off so just *save* it.

(Beat.)

CLAIRE: *(Smoothly, to* HAL*)* I'm Claire. Catherine's sister.

HAL: Oh, hi. Hal. Nice to meet you. *(Uncomfortable beat.)* I . . . hope it's not too early. I was just going to try to get some work done before the uh—if uh if . . .

CLAIRE: Yes!

CATHERINE: Sure, okay.

*(*HAL *exits. A moment.)*

CLAIRE: That's Harold Dobbs?

CATHERINE: Yes.

CLAIRE: He's cute.

CATHERINE: *(Disgusted)* Eugh.

CLAIRE: He's a mathematician?

CATHERINE: I think you owe me an apology, Claire.

CLAIRE: We need to make some decisions. But I shouldn't have tried to start first thing in the morning. I don't want an argument. *(Beat.)* Maybe Hal would like a bagel?

(Beat. CATHERINE *doesn't take the hint. She exits.)*

fade

Night. Inside the house a party is in progress. Loud music from a not-very-good but enthusiastic band. CATHERINE *is alone on the porch. She wears a flattering black dress. Inside, the band finishes a number. Cheers, applause. After a moment* HAL *comes out. He wears a dark suit. He has taken off his tie. He is sweaty and revved up from playing. He holds two bottles of beer.* CATHERINE *regards him. A beat.*

CATHERINE: I feel that for a funeral reception this might have gotten a bit out of control.

HAL: Aw come on. It's great. Come on in.

CATHERINE: I'm okay.

HAL: We're done playing, I promise.

CATHERINE: No thanks.

HAL: Do you want a beer?

CATHERINE: I'm okay.

HAL: I brought you one.

(Beat. CATHERINE *hesitates.)*

CATHERINE: Okay. *(She takes it, sips.)* How many people are in there?

HAL: It's down to about forty.

CATHERINE: Forty?

HAL: Just the hardcore partyers.

CATHERINE: My sister's friends.

HAL: No, mathematicians. Your sister's friends left hours ago. The guys were really pleased to be asked to participate. They worshipped your dad.

CATHERINE: It was Claire's idea.

HAL: It was good.

CATHERINE: *(Concedes)* The performance of "Imaginary Number" was . . . sort of . . . moving.

HAL: Good funeral. I mean not "good," but—

CATHERINE: No. Yeah.

HAL: Can you believe how many people came?

CATHERINE: I was surprised.

HAL: I think he would have liked it. (CATHERINE *looks at him.*) Sorry, it's not my place to—

CATHERINE: No, you're right. Everything was better than I thought.

(Beat.)

HAL: You look great.

CATHERINE: *(Indicates the dress)* Claire gave it to me.

HAL: I like it.

CATHERINE: It doesn't really fit.

HAL: No, Catherine, it's good.

(A moment. Noise from inside.)

CATHERINE: When do you think they'll leave?

HAL: No way to know. Mathematicians are insane. I went to this conference in Toronto last fall. I'm young, right? I'm in shape, I thought I could hang with the big boys. Wrong. I've never been so exhausted in my life. Forty-eight straight hours of partying, drinking, drugs, papers, lectures . . .

CATHERINE: Drugs?

HAL: Yeah. Amphetamines mostly. I mean, I don't. Some of the older guys are really hooked.

CATHERINE: Really?

HAL: Yeah, they think they need it.

CATHERINE: Why?

HAL: They think math's a young man's game. Speed keeps them racing, makes them feel sharp. There's this fear that your creativity peaks around twenty-three and it's all downhill from there. Once you hit fifty it's over, you might as well teach high school.

CATHERINE: That's what my father thought.

HAL: I dunno. Some people stay prolific.

CATHERINE: Not many.

HAL: No, you're right. Really original work—it's all young guys.

CATHERINE: Young guys.

HAL: Young people.

CATHERINE: But it is men, mostly.

HAL: There are some women.

CATHERINE: Who?

HAL: There's a woman at Stanford, I can't remember her name.

CATHERINE: Sophie Germain.

HAL: Yeah? I've probably seen her at meetings, I just don't think I've met her.

CATHERINE: She was born in Paris in 1776.

(Beat.)

HAL: So I've definitely never met her.

CATHERINE: She was trapped in her house.

The French Revolution was going on, the Terror. She had to stay inside for safety and she passed the time reading in her father's study. The Greeks . . . Later she tried to get a real education but the schools didn't allow women. So she wrote letters. She wrote to Gauss. She used a man's name. Uh—Antoine-August Le Blanc. She sent him some proofs involving a certain kind of prime number, important work. He was delighted to correspond with such a brilliant young man. Dad gave me a book about her.

HAL: I'm stupid. Sophie Germain, of course.

CATHERINE: You know her?

HAL: Germain Primes.

CATHERINE: Right.

HAL: They're famous. Double them and add one, and you get another prime. Like two. Two is prime, doubled plus one is five: also prime.

CATHERINE: Right. Or $92,305 \times 2^{16,998} + 1$.

HAL: *(Startled)* Right.

CATHERINE: That's the biggest one. The biggest one known . . .

(*Beat.*)

HAL: Did he ever find out who she was? Gauss.

CATHERINE: Yeah. Later a mutual friend told him the brilliant young man was a woman.

He wrote to her: "A taste for the mysteries of numbers is excessively rare, but when a person of the sex which, according to our customs and prejudices, must encounter infinitely more difficulties than men to familiarize herself with these thorny researches, succeeds nevertheless in penetrating the most obscure parts of them, then without a doubt she must have the noblest courage, quite extraordinary talents, and superior genius."

(*Now self-conscious*) I memorized it . . .

(HAL *stares at her. He suddenly kisses her, then stops, embarrassed. He moves away.*)

HAL: Sorry. I'm a little drunk.

CATHERINE: It's okay. (*Uncomfortable beat.*) I'm sorry about yesterday. I wasn't helpful. About the work you're doing. Take as long as you need upstairs.

HAL: You were fine. I was pushy.

CATHERINE: I was awful.

HAL: No. My timing was terrible. Anyway, you're probably right.

CATHERINE: What?

HAL: About it being junk.

CATHERINE: (*Nods.*) Yes.

HAL: I read through a lot of stuff today, just skimming. Except for the book I stole—

CATHERINE: Oh God, I'm sorry about that.

HAL: No, you were right.

CATHERINE: I shouldn't have called the police.

HAL: It was my fault.

CATHERINE: No.

HAL: The point is, that book—I'm starting to think it's the only lucid one, really. And there's no math in it.

CATHERINE: No.

HAL: I mean, I'll keep reading, but if I don't find anything in a couple of days . . .

CATHERINE: Back to the drums.

HAL: Yeah.

CATHERINE: And your own research.

HAL: Such as it is.

CATHERINE: What's wrong with it?

HAL: It's not exactly setting the world on fire.

CATHERINE: Oh come on.

HAL: It sucks, basically.

CATHERINE: Harold.

HAL: My papers get turned down. For the right reasons—my stuff is trivial. The big ideas aren't there.

CATHERINE: It's not about big ideas. It's work. You've got to chip away at a problem.

HAL: That's not what your dad did.

CATHERINE: I think it was, in a way. He'd attack a question from the side, from some weird angle, sneak up on it, grind away at it. He was slogging. He was just so much faster than anyone else that from the outside it looked magical.

HAL: I don't know.

CATHERINE: I'm just guessing.

HAL: Plus the work was beautiful. You can read it for pleasure. It's streamlined: no wasted moves, like a ninety-five-mile-an-hour fastball. It's just . . . elegant.

CATHERINE: Yeah.

HAL: And that's what you can never duplicate. At least I can't. It's okay. At a certain point you realize it's not going to happen, you readjust your expectations. I enjoy teaching.

CATHERINE: You might come up with something.

HAL: I'm twenty-eight, remember? On the downhill slope.

CATHERINE: Have you tried speed? I've heard it helps.

HAL: *(Laughs.)* Yeah.

(Beat.)

CATHERINE: So, Hal.

HAL: Yeah?

CATHERINE: What do you do for sex?

HAL: What?

CATHERINE: At your conferences.

HAL: Uh, I uh—

CATHERINE: Isn't that why people hold conferences? Travel. Room service. Tax-deductible sex in big hotel beds.

HAL: *(Laughs, nervous)* Maybe. I don't know.

CATHERINE: So what do you do? All you guys.

(Beat. Is she flirting with him? HAL is not sure.)

HAL: Well we are scientists.

CATHERINE: So?

HAL: So there's a lot of experimentation.

CATHERINE: *(Laughs.)* I see.

(Beat. CATHERINE goes to him. She kisses him. A longer kiss. It ends. HAL is surprised and pleased.)

HAL: Huh.

CATHERINE: That was nice.

HAL: Really?

CATHERINE: Yes.

HAL: Again?

CATHERINE: Yes.

(Kiss.)

HAL: I always liked you.

CATHERINE: You did?

HAL: Even before I knew you. I'd catch glimpses of you when you visited your dad's office at school. I wanted to talk to you, but I thought, No, you do not flirt with your doctoral adviser's daughter.

CATHERINE: Especially when your adviser's crazy.

HAL: Especially then.

(Kiss.)

CATHERINE: You came here once. Four years ago. Remember?

HAL: Sure. I can't believe you do. I was dropping off a draft of my thesis for your dad. Jesus I was nervous.

CATHERINE: You looked nervous.

HAL: I can't believe you remember that.

CATHERINE: I remember you. *(Kiss.)* I thought you seemed . . . not boring.

(They continue to kiss.)

fade

Scene 4

The next morning. CATHERINE *alone on the porch, in a robe.* HAL *enters, half-dressed. He walks up behind her quietly. She hears him and turns.*

HAL: How long have you been up?

CATHERINE: A while.

HAL: Did I oversleep?

CATHERINE: No.

(Beat. Morning-after awkwardness.)

HAL: Is your sister up?

CATHERINE: No. She's flying home in a couple hours. I should probably wake her.

HAL: Let her sleep. She was doing some pretty serious drinking with the theoretical physicists last night.

CATHERINE: I'll make her some coffee when she gets up.

(Beat.)

HAL: Sunday mornings I usually go out. Get the paper, have some breakfast.

CATHERINE: Okay.

(Beat.)

HAL: Do you want to come?

CATHERINE: Oh. No. I ought to stick around until Claire leaves.

HAL: All right. Do you mind if I stay?

CATHERINE: No. You can work if you want.

HAL: *(Taken aback)* Okay.

CATHERINE: Okay.

HAL: Should I?

CATHERINE: If you want to.

HAL: Do you want me to go?

CATHERINE: Do you want to go?

HAL: I want to stay here with you.

CATHERINE: Oh . . .

HAL: I want to spend the day with you if possible. I'd like to spend as much time with you as I can unless of course I'm coming on *way* too strong right now and scaring you in which case I'll begin backpedaling immediately . . . (CATHERINE *laughs. Her relief is evident; so is his. They kiss.*) How embarrassing is it if I say last night was wonderful?

CATHERINE: It's only embarrassing if I don't agree.

HAL: Uh, so . . .

CATHERINE: Don't be embarrassed. *(They kiss. After a moment she breaks off. She hesitates, making a decision. Then she takes a chain from around her neck. There is a key on the chain. She tosses it to* HAL.*)* Here.

HAL: What's this?

CATHERINE: It's a key.

HAL: Ah.

CATHERINE: Try it.

HAL: Where?

CATHERINE: Bottom drawer of the desk in my dad's office.

HAL: What's in there?

CATHERINE: There's one way to find out, Professor.

HAL: Now? (CATHERINE *shrugs. He laughs, unsure if this is a joke or not.*) Okay.

(HAL *kisses her quickly, then goes inside.* CATHERINE *smiles to herself. She is happy, on the edge of being giddy.* CLAIRE *enters, hungover. She sits down, squinting.*)

CATHERINE: Good morning.

CLAIRE: Please don't yell please.

CATHERINE: Are you all right?

CLAIRE: No. (*Beat. She clutches her head.*) Those fucking physicists.

CATHERINE: What happened?

CLAIRE: Thanks a *lot* for leaving me all alone with them.

CATHERINE: Where were your friends?

CLAIRE: My stupid friends left—it was only eleven o'clock!—they all had to get home and pay their babysitters or bake bread or something. I'm left alone with these lunatics . . .

CATHERINE: Why did you drink so much?

CLAIRE: I thought I could keep up with them. I thought they'd stop. They didn't. Oh God. "Have another tequila . . ."

CATHERINE: Do you want some coffee?

CLAIRE: In a minute. (*Beat.*) That *band.*

CATHERINE: Yeah.

CLAIRE: They were terrible.

CATHERINE: They were okay. They had fun. I think.

CLAIRE: Well as long as everyone had fun. (*Beat.*) Your dress turned out all right.

CATHERINE: I love it.

CLAIRE: You do.

CATHERINE: Yeah, it's wonderful.

CLAIRE: I was surprised you even wore it.

CATHERINE: I love it, Claire. Thanks.

CLAIRE: *(Surprised)* You're welcome. You're in a good mood.

CATHERINE: Should I not be?

CLAIRE: Are you kidding? No. I'm thrilled. *(Beat.)* I'm leaving in a few hours.

CATHERINE: I know.

CLAIRE: The house is a wreck. Don't clean it up yourself. I'll hire someone to come in.

CATHERINE: Thanks. You want your coffee?

CLAIRE: No, thanks.

CATHERINE: *(Starting in)* It's no trouble.

CLAIRE: Hold on a sec, Katie. I just . . . *(She takes a breath.)* I'm leaving soon. I—

CATHERINE: You said. I know.

CLAIRE: I'd still like you to come to New York.

CATHERINE: Yes: January.

CLAIRE: I'd like you to move to New York.

CATHERINE: Move?

CLAIRE: Would you think about it? For me? You could stay with me and Mitch at first. There's plenty of room. Then you could get your own place. I've already scouted some apartments for you, really cute places.

CATHERINE: What would I do in New York?

CLAIRE: What are you doing here?

CATHERINE: I live here.

CLAIRE: You could do whatever you want. You could work, you could go to school.

CATHERINE: I don't know, Claire. This is pretty major.

CLAIRE: I realize that.

CATHERINE: I know you mean well. I'm just not sure what I want to do. I mean to be honest you were right yesterday. I do feel a little confused. I'm tired. It's been a pretty weird couple of years. I think I'd like to take some time to figure things out.

CLAIRE: You could do that in New York.

CATHERINE: And I could do it here.

CLAIRE: But it would be much easier for me to get you set up in an apartment in New York, and—

CATHERINE: I don't need an apartment, I'll stay in the house.

CLAIRE: We're selling the house.

(Beat.)

CATHERINE: What?

CLAIRE: We—I'm selling it.

CATHERINE: *When?*

CLAIRE: I'm hoping to do the paperwork this week. I know it seems sudden.

CATHERINE: No one was here looking at the place, who are you selling it to?

CLAIRE: The university. They've wanted the block for years.

CATHERINE: *I live here.*

CLAIRE: Honey, now that Dad's gone it doesn't make sense. It's in bad shape. It costs a fortune to heat. It's time to let it go. Mitch agrees, it's a very smart move. We're lucky, we have a great offer—

CATHERINE: Where am I supposed to live?

CLAIRE: Come to New York.

CATHERINE: I can't believe this.

CLAIRE: It'll be so good. You deserve a change. This would be a whole new adventure for you.

CATHERINE: Why are you doing this?

CLAIRE: I want to help.

CATHERINE: By kicking me out of my *house?*

CLAIRE: It was my house too.

CATHERINE: You haven't lived here for years.

CLAIRE: I know that. You were on your own. I really regret that, Katie.

CATHERINE: Don't.

CLAIRE: I know I let you down. I feel awful about it. Now I'm trying to help.

CATHERINE: You want to help *now*?

CLAIRE: Yes.

CATHERINE: Dad is dead.

CLAIRE: I know.

CATHERINE: He's dead. Now that he's dead you fly in for the weekend and decide you want to help? *You're late.* Where have you been?

CLAIRE: I—

CATHERINE: Where were you five years ago? You weren't helping then.

CLAIRE: I was working.

CATHERINE: I was *here*. I lived with him *alone*.

CLAIRE: I was working fourteen-hour days. I paid every bill here. I paid off the mortgage on this three-bedroom house while I was living in a studio in Brooklyn.

CATHERINE: You had your life. You got to finish school.

CLAIRE: You could have stayed in school!

CATHERINE: How?

CLAIRE: I would have done anything—I told you that. I told you a million times to do anything you wanted.

CATHERINE: What about Dad? Someone had to take care of him.

CLAIRE: He was ill. He should have been in a full-time professional-care situation.

CATHERINE: He didn't belong in the nuthouse.

CLAIRE: He might have been better off.

CATHERINE: How can you say that?

CLAIRE: This is where I'm meant to feel guilty, right?

CATHERINE: Sure, go for it.

CLAIRE: I'm heartless. My own father.

CATHERINE: He needed to be here. In his own house, near the university, near his students, near everything that made him happy.

CLAIRE: Maybe. Or maybe some real professional care would have done him more good than rattling around in a filthy house with *you* looking after him.

I'm sorry, Catherine, it's not your fault. It's my fault for letting you do it.

CATHERINE: I was right to keep him here.

CLAIRE: No.

CATHERINE: What about his remission? Four years ago. He was healthy for almost a year.

CLAIRE: And then he went right downhill again.

CATHERINE: He might have been worse in a hospital.

CLAIRE: And he *might* have been *better*. Did he ever do any work again?

CATHERINE: No.

CLAIRE: *No. (Beat.)* And you might have been better.

CATHERINE: *(Keeping her voice under control)* Better than what?

CLAIRE: Living here with him didn't do you any good. You said that yourself.

You had so much talent . . .

CATHERINE: You think I'm like Dad.

CLAIRE: I think you have some of his talent and some of his tendency toward . . . instability.

(Beat.)

CATHERINE: Claire, in addition to the "cute apartments" that you've "scouted" for me in New York, would you by any chance also have devoted some of your considerable energies toward scouting out another type of—

CLAIRE: *No.*

CATHERINE: —living facility for your bughouse little sister?

CLAIRE: *No!* Absolutely not. That is not what this is about.

CATHERINE: Don't lie to me, Claire. I'm smarter than you.

(Beat.)

CLAIRE: The resources . . . I've investigated—

CATHERINE: Oh my *God*.

CLAIRE: —if you *wanted* to, all I'm saying is, the doctors in New York and the people are the *best*, and they—

CATHERINE: *Fuck you.*

CLAIRE: It would be entirely up to you. You wouldn't *live* anywhere, you can—

CATHERINE: I hate you.

CLAIRE: Don't yell, please. Calm down.

CATHERINE: *I hate you.* I—

(HAL *enters, holding a notebook.* CLAIRE *and* CATHERINE *stop suddenly. Beat.*)

CLAIRE: What are you doing here? . . .

(CLAIRE *stares at* CATHERINE.)

HAL: How long have you known about this?

CATHERINE: A while.

HAL: Why didn't you tell me about it?

CATHERINE: I wasn't sure I wanted to.

(*Beat.*)

HAL: Thank you.

CATHERINE: You're welcome.

CLAIRE: What's going on?

HAL: God, Catherine, thank you.

CATHERINE: I thought you'd like to see it.

CLAIRE: What is it?

HAL: It's incredible.

CLAIRE: What *is* it?

HAL: Oh, uh, it's a result. A proof. I mean it looks like a proof. I mean it is a proof, a very long proof, I haven't read it all of course, or checked it, I don't even know if I *could* check it, but if it *is* a proof of what I think it's a proof of, it's . . . a very . . . *important* . . . proof.

CLAIRE: What does it prove?

HAL: It looks like it proves a theorem . . . a mathematical theorem about prime numbers, something mathematicians have been trying to prove since . . . since there were mathematicians, basically. Most people thought it couldn't be done.

CLAIRE: Where did you find it?

HAL: In your father's desk. Cathy told me about it.

CLAIRE: You know what this is?

CATHERINE: Sure.

CLAIRE: Is it good?

CATHERINE: Yes.

HAL: It's historic. If it checks out.

CLAIRE: What does it say?

HAL: I don't know yet. I've just read the first few pages.

CLAIRE: But what does it mean?

HAL: It means that during a time when everyone thought your dad was crazy . . . or barely functioning . . . he was doing some of the most important mathematics in the world. If it checks out, it means you publish instantly. It means newspapers all over the world are going to want to talk to the person who found this notebook.

CLAIRE: Cathy.

HAL: Cathy.

CATHERINE: I didn't find it.

HAL: Yes you did.

CATHERINE: No.

CLAIRE: Well did you find it or did Hal find it?

HAL: I didn't find it.

CATHERINE: I didn't find it.

I wrote it.

Curtain

Act Two

Scene 1

ROBERT *is alone on the porch. He sits quietly, enjoying a drink, the quiet, the September afternoon. A notebook nearby, unopened. He closes his eyes, apparently dozing. It is four years earlier than the events in Act One.* CATHERINE *enters quietly. She stands behind her father for a moment.*

ROBERT: Hello.
CATHERINE: How did you know I was here?
ROBERT: I heard you.
CATHERINE: I thought you were asleep.
ROBERT: On an afternoon like this? No.
CATHERINE: Do you need anything?
ROBERT: No.
CATHERINE: I'm going to the store.
ROBERT: What's for dinner?
CATHERINE: What do you want?
ROBERT: Not spaghetti.
CATHERINE: All right.
ROBERT: Disgusting stuff.
CATHERINE: That's what I was going to make.
ROBERT: I had a feeling. Good thing I spoke up. You make it too much.
CATHERINE: What do you want?

ROBERT: What do you have a taste for?

CATHERINE: Nothing.

ROBERT: Nothing at all?

CATHERINE: I don't care. I thought pasta would be easy.

ROBERT: Pasta, oh God, don't even say the word "pasta." It sounds so hopeless, like surrender: "Pasta would be easy." Yes, yes, it would. Pasta. It doesn't *mean* anything. It's just a euphemism people invented when they got sick of eating spaghetti.

CATHERINE: Dad, what do you want to eat?

ROBERT: I don't know.

CATHERINE: Well I don't know what to get.

ROBERT: I'll shop.

CATHERINE: No.

ROBERT: I'll do it.

CATHERINE: No, Dad, rest.

ROBERT: I wanted to take a walk anyway.

CATHERINE: Are you sure?

ROBERT: Yes. What about a walk to the lake? You and me.

CATHERINE: All right.

ROBERT: I would love to go to the lake. Then on the way home we'll stop at the store, see what jumps out at us.

CATHERINE: It's warm. It would be nice, if you're up for it.

ROBERT: You're damn right I'm up for it. We'll work up an appetite. Give me ten seconds, let me put this stuff away and we're out the door.

CATHERINE: I'm going to school.

(*Beat.*)

ROBERT: When?

CATHERINE: I'm gonna start at Northwestern at the end of the month.

ROBERT: Northwestern?

CATHERINE: They were great about my credits. They're taking

me in as a sophomore. I wasn't sure when to talk to you about it.

ROBERT: Northwestern?

CATHERINE: Yes.

ROBERT: What's wrong with Chicago?

CATHERINE: You still teach there. I'm sorry, it's too weird, taking classes in your department.

ROBERT: It's a long drive.

CATHERINE: Not that long, half an hour.

ROBERT: Still, twice a day . . .

CATHERINE: Dad, I'd live there.

(Beat.)

ROBERT: You'd actually want to live in Evanston?

CATHERINE: Yes. I'll still be close. I can come home whenever you want.

You've been well—really well—for almost seven months. I don't think you need me here every minute of the day.

(Beat.)

ROBERT: This is all a done deal? You're in.

CATHERINE: Yes.

ROBERT: You're sure.

CATHERINE: *Yes.*

ROBERT: Who pays for it?

CATHERINE: They're giving me a free ride, Dad. They've been great.

ROBERT: On tuition, sure. What about food, books, clothes, gas, meals out—do you plan to have a social life?

CATHERINE: I don't know.

ROBERT: You gotta pay your own way on dates, at least the early dates, say the first three, otherwise they expect something.

CATHERINE: The money will be fine. Claire's gonna help out.

ROBERT: When did you talk to Claire?

CATHERINE: I don't know, a couple weeks ago.

ROBERT: You talk to her before you talk to me?

CATHERINE: There were a lot of details to work out. She was great, she offered to take care of all the expenses.

ROBERT: This is a big step. A different *city*—

CATHERINE: It's not even a long-distance phone call.

ROBERT: It's a huge place. They're serious up there. I mean serious. Yeah the football's a disaster but the math guys don't kid around. You haven't been in school. You sure you're ready? You can get buried up there.

CATHERINE: I'll be all right.

ROBERT: You're way behind.

CATHERINE: I know.

ROBERT: A year, at least.

CATHERINE: Thank you, *I know.* Look, I don't know if this is a good idea. I don't know if I can handle the work. I don't know if I can handle *any* of it.

ROBERT: For Chrissake, Catherine, you should have talked to me.

CATHERINE: Dad. Listen. If you ever . . . if for any reason it ever turned out that you needed me here full-time again—

ROBERT: *I won't.* That's not—

CATHERINE: I can always take a semester off, or—

ROBERT: No. Stop it. I just—the end of the *month*? Why didn't you say something before?

CATHERINE: Dad, come on. It took a while to set this up, and until recently, until very recently, you weren't—

ROBERT: You just said yourself I've been fine.

CATHERINE: Yes, but I didn't know—*I hoped*, but I didn't *know*, no one knew if this would last. I told myself to wait until I was sure about you. That you were feeling okay again. Consistently okay.

ROBERT: So I'm to take this conversation as a vote of confidence? I'm honored.

CATHERINE: Take it however you want. I believed you'd get better.

ROBERT: Well thank you very much.

CATHERINE: Don't thank me. I had to. I was living with you.

ROBERT: All right, that's enough, Catherine. Let's stay on the subject.

CATHERINE: This is the subject! There were *library books* upstairs stacked up to the ceiling, do you remember that? You were trying to decode *messages*—

ROBERT: The fucking books are gone, I took them back myself. Why do you bring that garbage up?

(Knocking offstage. Beat. CATHERINE *goes inside to answer the door. She returns with* HAL. *He carries a manila envelope. He is nervous.)*

ROBERT: Mr. Dobbs.

HAL: Hi. I hope it's not a bad time.

ROBERT: Yes it is, actually, you couldn't have picked worse.

HAL: Oh, I uh—

ROBERT: You interrupted an argument.

HAL: I'm sorry. I can come back.

ROBERT: It's all right. We needed a break.

HAL: Are you sure?

ROBERT: Yes. The argument was about dinner. We don't know what to eat. What's your suggestion?

(A beat while HAL *is on the spot.)*

HAL: Uh, there's a great pasta place not too far from here.

ROBERT: *No!*

CATHERINE *(with* ROBERT*)*: That is a *brilliant* idea.

ROBERT: Oh dear Jesus God, no.

CATHERINE *(with* ROBERT*)*: What's it called? Give me the address.

ROBERT: No! Sorry. Wrong answer, but thank you for trying.

*(*HAL *stands there, looking at both of them.)*

HAL: I can come back.

ROBERT: Stay. *(To* CATHERINE*)* Where are you going?

CATHERINE: Inside.

ROBERT: What about dinner?

CATHERINE: What about him?

ROBERT: What are you doing here, Dobbs?

HAL: My timing sucks. I am really sorry.

ROBERT: Don't be silly.

HAL: I'll come to your office.

ROBERT: Stop. Sit down. Glad you're here. Don't let the dinner thing throw you, you'll bounce back. *(To* CATHERINE*)* This should be easier. Let's back off the problem, let it breathe, come at it again when it's not looking.

CATHERINE: Fine. *(Exiting)* Excuse me.

ROBERT: Sorry, I'm rude. Hal, this is my daughter Catherine. *(To* CATHERINE*)* Don't go, have a drink with us. Catherine, Harold Dobbs.

CATHERINE: Hi.

HAL: Hi.

ROBERT: Hal is a grad student. He's doing his Ph.D., very promising stuff. Unfortunately for him, his work coincided with my return to the department and he got stuck with me.

HAL: No, no, it's been— I've been very lucky.

CATHERINE: How long have you been at U. of C.?

HAL: Well I've been working on my thesis for—

ROBERT: Hal's in our "Infinite" program. As he approaches completion of his dissertation, time approaches infinity. Would you like a drink, Hal?

HAL: Yes I would. And uh, with all due respect . . .

*(*HAL *hands* ROBERT *the envelope.)*

ROBERT: Really? *(He opens it and looks inside.)* You must have had an interesting few months.

HAL: *(Cheerfully)* Worst summer of my life.

ROBERT: Congratulations.

HAL: It's just a draft. Based on everything we talked about last spring. *(ROBERT pours a drink.* HAL *babbles.)* I wasn't sure if I should wait till the quarter started, or if I should give it to you *now*, or hold off, do another draft, but I figured fuck it, I, I mean I just . . . let's just get it *over* with, so I thought I'd just come over and see if you were home, and—

ROBERT: Drink this.

HAL: Thanks. *(He drinks.)* I decided, I don't know, if it feels done, maybe it is.

ROBERT: Wrong. If it feels done, there are major errors.

HAL: Uh, I—

ROBERT: That's okay, that's good, we'll find them and fix them. Don't worry. You're on your way to a solid career, you'll be teaching younger, more irritating versions of yourself in no time.

HAL: Thank you.

ROBERT: Catherine's in the math department at Northwestern, Hal.

(CATHERINE looks up, startled.)

HAL: Oh, who are you working with?

CATHERINE: I'm just starting this fall. Undergrad.

ROBERT: She's starting in . . . three weeks?

CATHERINE: A little more.

(Beat.)

ROBERT: They have some good people at Northwestern. O'Donohue. Kaminsky.

CATHERINE: Yes.

ROBERT: They will work your ass off.

CATHERINE: I know.

ROBERT: You'll have to run pretty hard to catch up.

CATHERINE: I think I can do it.

ROBERT: Of course you can. *(Beat.)*

HAL: You must be excited.

CATHERINE: I am.

HAL: First year of school can be great.

CATHERINE: Yeah?

HAL: Sure, all the new people, new places, getting out of the house.

CATHERINE: *(Embarrassed)* Yes.

HAL: *(Embarrassed)* Or, no, I—

ROBERT: Absolutely, getting the hell out of here, thank God, it's about time. I'll be glad to see the back of her.

CATHERINE: You will?

ROBERT: Of course. Maybe I want to have the place to myself for a while, did that ever occur to you? *(To* HAL*)* It's awful the way children sentimentalize their parents. *(To* CATHERINE*)* We could use some quiet around here.

CATHERINE: Oh don't worry, I'll come back. I'll be here every Sunday cooking up big vats of pasta to last you through the week.

ROBERT: And I'll drive up, strut around Evanston, embarrass you in front of your classmates.

CATHERINE: Good. So we'll be in touch.

ROBERT: Sure. And if you get stuck with a problem, give me a call.

CATHERINE: Okay. Same to you.

ROBERT: Fine. Make sure to get me your number. *(To* HAL*)* I'm actually looking forward to getting some work done.

HAL: Oh, what are you working on?

ROBERT: Nothing. *(Beat.)* Nothing at the moment.

Which I'm glad of, really. This is the time of year when you don't want to be tied down to anything. You want to be outside. I love Chicago in September. Perfect skies. Sailboats on the water. Cubs losing. Warm, the sun still hot . . . with the occasional blast of Arctic wind to keep you on your toes, remind you of winter. Students coming back, bookstores full, everybody busy.

I was in a bookstore yesterday. Completely full, students

buying books . . . browsing . . . Students do a hell of a lot of browsing, don't they? Just browsing. You see them shuffling around with their backpacks, goofing off, taking up space. You'd call it loitering except every once in a while they pick up a book and flip the pages: "browsing." I admire it. It's an honest way to kill an afternoon. In the back of a used bookstore, or going through a crate of somebody's old record albums—not looking for anything, just looking, what the hell, touching the old book jackets, seeing what somebody threw out, seeing what they underlined . . . Maybe you find something great, like an old thriller with a painted cover from the forties, or a textbook one of your professors used when *he* was a student—his name is written in it very carefully . . . Yeah, I like it. I like watching the students. Wondering what they're gonna buy, what they're gonna read. What kind of ideas they'll come up with when they settle down and get to work . . .

I'm not doing much right now. It does get harder. It's a stereotype that happens to be true, unfortunately for me— unfortunately for you, for all of us.

CATHERINE: Maybe you'll get lucky.

ROBERT: Maybe I will. Maybe you'll pick up where I left off.

CATHERINE: Don't hold your breath.

ROBERT: Don't underestimate yourself.

CATHERINE: Anyway.

(Beat.)

ROBERT: Another drink? Cathy? Hal?

CATHERINE: No thanks.

HAL: Thanks, I really should get going.

ROBERT: Are you sure?

HAL: Yes.

ROBERT: I'll call you when I've looked at this. Don't think about it till then. Enjoy yourself, see some movies.

HAL: Okay.

ROBERT: You can come by my office in a week. Call it—

HAL: The eleventh?

ROBERT: Yes, we'll . . . *(Beat. He turns to* CATHERINE. *Grave)* I am sorry. I used to have a pretty good memory for numbers. Happy birthday.

CATHERINE: Thank you.

ROBERT: I am so sorry. I'm embarrassed.

CATHERINE: Dad, don't be stupid.

ROBERT: I didn't get you anything.

CATHERINE: Don't worry about it.

ROBERT: I'm taking you out.

CATHERINE: You don't have to.

ROBERT: We are going out. I didn't want to shop and cook. Let's go to dinner. Let's get the hell out of this neighborhood. What do you want to eat? Let's go to the North Side. Or Chinatown. Or Greektown. I don't know what's good anymore.

CATHERINE: Whatever you want.

ROBERT: Whatever *you* want goddamnit, Catherine, it's your birthday.

(Beat.)

CATHERINE: Steak.

ROBERT: Steak. Yes.

CATHERINE: No, first beer, really cold beer. Really cheap beer.

ROBERT: Done.

CATHERINE: That Chicago beer that's watery with no flavor and you can just drink *gallons* of it.

ROBERT: They just pump the water out of Lake Michigan and bottle it.

CATHERINE: It's so awful.

ROBERT: I have a taste for it myself.

CATHERINE: Then the steak, grilled really black, and potatoes and creamed spinach.

ROBERT: I remember a place. If it's still there I think it will do the trick.

CATHERINE: And dessert.

ROBERT: That goes without saying. It's your birthday, hooray. And there's the solution to our dinner problem. Thank you for reminding me, Harold Dobbs.

CATHERINE: *(To* HAL*)* We're being rude. Do you want to come?

HAL: Oh, no, I shouldn't.

ROBERT: Why not? Please, come.

CATHERINE: Come on.

(A tiny moment between HAL *and* CATHERINE. HAL *wavers, then)*

HAL: No, I can't, I have plans. Thank you, though. Happy birthday.

CATHERINE: Thanks. Well. I'll let you out.

ROBERT: I'll see you on the eleventh, Hal.

HAL: Great.

CATHERINE: I'm gonna change my clothes, Dad. I'll be ready in a sec.

*(*HAL *and* CATHERINE *exit. A moment. It's darker.* ROBERT *looks out at the evening. Eventually he picks up the notebook and a pen. He sits down. He opens to a blank page. He writes.)*

ROBERT: "September fourth. A good day . . ." *(He continues to write.)*

fade

Scene 2

Morning. An instant after the end of Act One: CATHERINE, CLAIRE, *and* HAL.

HAL: You wrote this?

CATHERINE: Yes.

CLAIRE: When?

CATHERINE: I started after I quit school. I finished a few months before Dad died.

CLAIRE: Did he see it?

CATHERINE: No. He didn't know I was working on it. It wouldn't have mattered to him anyway, he was too sick.

HAL: I don't understand—you did this by yourself?

CATHERINE: *Yes.*

CLAIRE: It's in Dad's notebook.

CATHERINE: I used one of his blank books. There were a bunch of them upstairs.

(Beat.)

CLAIRE: *(To* HAL*)* Tell me exactly where you found this.

HAL: In his study.

CATHERINE: In his desk. I gave him the—

CLAIRE: *(To* CATHERINE*)* Hold on. *(To* HAL*)* Where did you find it?

HAL: In the bottom drawer of the desk in the study, a locked drawer: Catherine gave me the key.

CLAIRE: Why was the drawer locked?

CATHERINE: It's mine, it's the drawer I keep my private things in. I've used it for years.

CLAIRE: *(To* HAL*)* Was there anything else in the drawer?

HAL: No.

CATHERINE: No, that's the only—

CLAIRE: Can I see it? *(*HAL *gives* CLAIRE *the book. She pages through it. Beat.)* I'm sorry, I just . . . *(To* CATHERINE*)* The book was in the . . . You told him where to find it . . . You gave him the key . . . You wrote this incredible thing and you didn't *tell* anyone?

CATHERINE: I'm telling you both now. After I dropped out of school I had nothing to do. I was depressed, really depressed, but at a certain point I decided, Fuck it, I don't need them. It's just math, I can do it on my own. So I kept

working here. I worked at night, after Dad had gone to
sleep. It was hard but I did it.

(Beat.)

CLAIRE: Catherine, I'm sorry but I just find this very hard to
believe.

CATHERINE: Claire. I wrote. The proof.

CLAIRE: I'm sorry, I—

CATHERINE: Claire . . .

CLAIRE: This is Dad's handwriting.

CATHERINE: It's not.

CLAIRE: It looks exactly like it.

CATHERINE: It's my writing.

CLAIRE: I'm sorry—

CATHERINE: Ask Hal, he's been looking at Dad's writing for
weeks.

*(*CLAIRE *gives* HAL *the book. He looks at it. Beat.)*

HAL: I don't know.

CATHERINE: Hal, come on.

CLAIRE: What does it look like?

HAL: It looks . . . I don't know what Catherine's handwriting
looks like.

CATHERINE: It *looks* like *that*.

HAL: Okay. It . . . Okay. *(Beat. He hands the book back.)*

CLAIRE: I think—you know what? I think it's early, and people are tired and not in the best state to make decisions
about emotional things, so maybe we should all just take a
breath . . .

CATHERINE: You don't believe me?

CLAIRE: I don't know. I really don't know anything about this.

CATHERINE: Never mind. I don't know why I expected you to
believe me about *anything*.

CLAIRE: Could you *tell* us the proof? That would show it was
yours.

CATHERINE: You wouldn't understand it.

CLAIRE: Tell it to Hal.

CATHERINE: *(Taking the book)* We could talk through it together. It might take a while.

CLAIRE: *(Taking the book)* You can't use the book.

CATHERINE: For God's sake, it's forty pages long. I didn't *memorize* it. It's not a muffin recipe.

This is stupid. It's my book, my writing, my key, my drawer, my proof. Hal, tell her!

HAL: Tell her what?

CATHERINE: Whose book is that?

HAL: I don't know.

CATHERINE: What is the matter with you? You've been looking at his other stuff, you know there's nothing even remotely like this!

HAL: Look, Catherine—

CATHERINE: We'll go through the proof together. We'll sit down—if Claire will *please* let me have my book back—

CLAIRE: *(Giving her the book)* All right, talk him through it.

HAL: That might take days and it still wouldn't show that she wrote it.

CATHERINE: Why not?

HAL: Your dad might have written it and explained it to you later. I'm not saying he did, I'm just saying there's no proof that you wrote this.

CATHERINE: Of course there isn't, but come on! He didn't do this, he couldn't have. He didn't do any mathematics at all for years. Even in the good year he couldn't work: you *know* that. You're supposed to be a scientist.

(Beat.)

HAL: You're right. Okay. Here's my suggestion. I know three or four guys at the department, very sharp, disinterested people who knew your father, knew his work. Let me take this to them.

CATHERINE: What?

HAL: I'll tell them we've found something, something potentially major, we're not sure about the authorship; I'll sit down with them. We'll go through the thing carefully—

CLAIRE: Good.

HAL: —and figure out exactly what we've got. It would only take a couple of days, probably, and then we'd have a lot more information.

CLAIRE: I think that's an excellent suggestion.

CATHERINE: You can't.

CLAIRE: Catherine.

CATHERINE: No! You can't take it.

HAL: I'm not "taking" it.

CATHERINE: This is what you wanted.

HAL: Oh come on, Jesus.

CATHERINE: You don't waste any time, do you? No hesitation. You can't wait to show them your brilliant discovery.

HAL: I'm trying to determine what this is.

CATHERINE: I'm telling you what it is.

HAL: You don't know!

CATHERINE: *I wrote it.*

HAL: *It's your father's handwriting. (Beat. Pained)* At least it looks an awful lot like the writing in the other books. Maybe your writing looks exactly like his, I don't know.

CATHERINE: *(Softly)* It does look like his.

I didn't show this to anyone else. I could have. I wanted you to be the first to see it. I didn't know I wanted that until last night. It's *me*. I trusted you.

HAL: I know.

CATHERINE: Was I wrong?

HAL: No. I—

CATHERINE: I should have known she wouldn't believe me but why don't you?

HAL: This is one of his notebooks. The exact same kind he used.

CATHERINE: I told you. I just used one of his blank books. There were extras.

HAL: There aren't any extra books in the study.

CATHERINE: There were when I started writing the proof. I bought them for him. He must have used the rest up later.

HAL: And the writing.

CATHERINE: You want to test the handwriting?

HAL: No. It doesn't matter. He could have dictated it to you for Chrissake. It still doesn't make sense.

CATHERINE: Why not?

HAL: I'm a mathematician.

CATHERINE: Yes.

HAL: I know how hard it would be to come up with something like this. I mean it's impossible. You'd have to be . . . you'd have to be your dad, basically. Your dad at the peak of his powers.

CATHERINE: I'm a mathematician too.

HAL: Not like your dad.

CATHERINE: Oh, he's the only one who could have done this?

HAL: The only one I know.

CATHERINE: Are you sure?

HAL: Your father was the most—

CATHERINE: Just because you and the rest of the geeks worshipped him doesn't mean he wrote this proof, Hal!

HAL: He was the *best*. My generation hasn't produced anything like him. He revolutionized the field twice before he was twenty-two. I'm sorry, Catherine, but you took some classes at Northwestern for a few months.

CATHERINE: My education wasn't at Northwestern. It was living in this house for twenty-five years.

HAL: Even so, it doesn't matter. This is too advanced. I don't even understand most of it.

CATHERINE: You think it's too advanced.

HAL: Yes.

CATHERINE: It's too advanced for *you*.

HAL: You could not have done this work.

CATHERINE: But what if I did?

HAL: Well what if?

CATHERINE: It would be a real disaster for you, wouldn't it? And for the other geeks who *barely* finished their Ph.D.'s, who are marking time doing *lame* research, bragging about the conferences they go to—*wow*—playing in an *awful* band, and whining that they're intellectually past it at twenty-eight, *because they are.*

(*Beat.* HAL *hesitates, then abruptly exits. Beat.* CATHERINE *is furious and so upset she looks dazed.*)

CLAIRE: Katie. Let's go inside. Katie?

(CATHERINE *opens the book, tries to rip out the pages, destroy it.* CLAIRE *goes to take it from her. They struggle.* CATHERINE *gets the book away. They stand apart, breathing hard. After a moment,* CATHERINE *throws the book to the floor. She exits.*)

fade

Scene 3

The next day. The porch is empty. Knocking off. No one appears. After a moment HAL *comes around the side of the porch and knocks on the back door.*

HAL: Catherine?

(CLAIRE *enters.*)

HAL: I thought you were leaving.

CLAIRE: I had to delay my flight.

(*Beat.*)

HAL: Is Catherine here?

CLAIRE: I don't think this is a good time, Hal.

HAL: Could I see her?

CLAIRE: Not now.

HAL: What's the matter?

CLAIRE: She's sleeping.

HAL: Can I wait here until she gets up?

CLAIRE: She's been sleeping since yesterday. She won't get up. She won't eat, won't talk to me. I couldn't go home. I'm going to wait until she seems okay to travel.

HAL: Jesus, I'm sorry.

CLAIRE: Yes.

HAL: I'd like to talk to her.

CLAIRE: I don't think that's a good idea.

HAL: Has she said anything?

CLAIRE: About you? No.

HAL: Yesterday . . . I know I didn't do what she wanted.

CLAIRE: Neither of us did.

HAL: I didn't know what to say. I feel awful.

CLAIRE: Why did you sleep with her?

(Beat.)

HAL: I'm sorry, that's none of your business.

CLAIRE: Bullshit. I have to take care of her. It's a little bit harder with you jerking her around.

HAL: I wasn't jerking her around. It just happened.

CLAIRE: Your timing was not great.

HAL: It wasn't *my* timing, it was *both* of our—

CLAIRE: Why'd you do it? You know what she's like. She's fragile and you took advantage of her.

HAL: No. It's what we both wanted. I didn't mean to hurt her.

CLAIRE: You did.

HAL: I'd like to talk to Catherine, please.

CLAIRE: You can't.

HAL: Are you taking her away?

CLAIRE: Yes.

HAL: To New York.

CLAIRE: Yes.

HAL: Just going to drag her to New York.

CLAIRE: If I have to.

HAL: Don't you think she should have some say in whether or not she goes?

CLAIRE: If she's not going to speak, what else can I do?

HAL: Let me try. Let me talk to her.

CLAIRE: Hal, give up. This has nothing to do with you.

HAL: I know her. She's tougher than you think, Claire.

CLAIRE: What?

HAL: She can handle herself. She can handle talking to me— maybe it would help. Maybe she'd like it.

CLAIRE: Maybe she'd *like* it? Are you out of your *mind*? You're the reason she's up there right now! You have *no idea* what she needs. You don't know her! She's my sister. Jesus, you fucking mathematicians: you *don't think*. You don't know what you're doing. You stagger around creating these catastrophes and it's people like me who end up flying in to clean them up. *(Beat.)* She needs to get out of Chicago, out of this house. I'll give you my number in New York. You can call her once she's settled there. That's it, that's the deal.

HAL: Okay. *(Beat. He doesn't move.)*

CLAIRE: I don't mean to be rude but I have a lot to do.

HAL: There's one more thing. You're not going to like it.

CLAIRE: Sure, take the notebook.

HAL: *(Startled)* I—

CLAIRE: Hold on a sec, I'll get it for you. *(She goes inside and returns with the notebook. She gives it to HAL.)*

HAL: I thought this would be harder.

CLAIRE: Don't worry, I understand. It's very sweet you want to see Catherine but of course you'd like to see the notebook too.

HAL: *(Huffy)* It's— No, it's my responsibility—as a professional I can't turn my back on the necessity of the—

CLAIRE: Relax. I don't care. Take it. What would I do with it?

HAL: You sure?

CLAIRE: Yes, of course.

HAL: You trust me with this?

CLAIRE: Yes.

HAL: You just said I don't know what I'm doing.

CLAIRE: I think you're a little bit of an idiot but you're not dishonest. Someone needs to figure out what's in there. I can't do it. It should be done here, at Chicago: my father would like that. When you decide what we've got let me know what the family should do.

HAL: Thanks.

CLAIRE: Don't thank me, it's by far the most convenient option available. I put my card in there, call me whenever you want.

HAL: Okay.

(HAL *starts to exit.* CLAIRE *hesitates, then)*

CLAIRE: Hal.

HAL: Yeah?

CLAIRE: Can you tell me about it? The proof. I'm just curious.

HAL: It would take some time. How much math have you got?

(Beat.)

CLAIRE: I'm a currency analyst. It helps to be very quick with numbers. I am. I probably inherited about one one-thousandth of my father's ability. It's enough.

Catherine got more, I'm not sure how much.

fade

Scene 4

Winter. About three and a half years earlier. ROBERT *is on the porch. He wears a T-shirt. He writes in a notebook. After a moment we hear* CATHERINE'*s voice from offstage.*

CATHERINE: Dad? *(She enters wearing a parka. She sees her father and stops.)* What are you doing out here?

ROBERT: Working.

CATHERINE: It's December. It's thirty degrees.

ROBERT: I know.

*(*CATHERINE *stares at him, baffled.)*

CATHERINE: Don't you need a coat?

ROBERT: Don't you think I can make that assessment for myself? *(Beat.)*

CATHERINE: Aren't you cold?

ROBERT: Of course I am! I'm freezing my ass off!

CATHERINE: So what are you *doing* out here?

ROBERT: Thinking! Writing!

CATHERINE: You're gonna freeze.

ROBERT: It's too hot in the house. The radiators dry out the air. Also the clanking—I can't concentrate. If the house weren't so old, we'd have central air heating, but we don't, so I have to come out here to get any work done.

CATHERINE: I'll turn off the radiators. They won't make any noise. Come inside, it isn't safe.

ROBERT: I'm okay.

CATHERINE: I've been calling. Didn't you hear the phone?

ROBERT: It's a distraction.

CATHERINE: I didn't know what was going on. I had to drive all the way down here.

ROBERT: I can see that.

CATHERINE: I had to skip class. *(She brings* ROBERT *a coat and he puts it on.)* Why don't you answer the phone?

ROBERT: Well I'm sorry, Catherine, but it's a question of priorities, and work takes priority, you know that.

CATHERINE: You're working?

ROBERT: Goddamnit, I am working! I say "I"— The machinery. The machinery is working. Catherine, it's on full-blast. All the cylinders are firing, I'm on fire. That's why I came out here, to cool off. I haven't felt like this for years.

CATHERINE: You're kidding.

ROBERT: No!

CATHERINE: I don't believe it.

ROBERT: I don't believe it either! But it's true. It started about a week ago. I woke up, came downstairs, made a cup of coffee, and before I could pour in the milk it was like someone turned the *light* on in my head.

CATHERINE: Really?

ROBERT: Not the light, the whole *power grid. I lit up*, and it's like no time has passed since I was twenty-one.

CATHERINE: You're kidding!

ROBERT: No! I'm back! I'm back in touch with the source—the font, the—whatever the source of my creativity was all those years ago. I'm in contact with it again. I'm *sitting* on it. It's a geyser and I'm shooting right up into the air on top of it.

CATHERINE: My God.

ROBERT: I'm not talking about divine inspiration. It's not funneling down into my head and onto the page. It'll take *work* to shape these things; I'm not saying it won't be a tremendous amount of work. It *will* be a tremendous amount of work. It's not going to be easy. But the raw material is there. It's like I've been driving in traffic and now the lanes are opening up before me and I can *accelerate.* I see whole landscapes—places for the work to go, new techniques, revolutionary possibilities. I'm going to get whole branches of the profession talking to each other. I—I'm sorry, I'm being rude. How's school?

CATHERINE: *(Taken aback)* Fine.

ROBERT: You're working hard?

CATHERINE: Sure.

ROBERT: Faculty treating you all right?

CATHERINE: Yes. Dad—

ROBERT: Made any friends?

CATHERINE: Of course. I—

ROBERT: Dating?

CATHERINE: Dad, hold on.

ROBERT: No details necessary if you don't want to provide them. I'm just interested.

CATHERINE: School's great. I want to talk about what you're doing.

ROBERT: Great, let's talk.

CATHERINE: This work.

ROBERT: Yes.

CATHERINE: *(Indicating the notebooks)* Is it here?

ROBERT: Part of it, yes.

CATHERINE: Can I see it?

ROBERT: It's all at a very early stage.

CATHERINE: I don't mind.

ROBERT: Nothing's actually complete, to be honest. It's all in progress. I think we're talking years.

CATHERINE: That's okay. I don't care. Just let me see anything.

ROBERT: You really want to?

CATHERINE: Yes.

ROBERT: You're genuinely interested.

CATHERINE: Dad, of course!

ROBERT: Of course. It's your field.

CATHERINE: Yes.

ROBERT: You know how happy that makes me.

(*Beat.*)

CATHERINE: Yes.

ROBERT: I think there's enough here to keep me working the rest of my life.

Not just me.

I was starting to imagine I was finished, Catherine. Really finished. Don't get me wrong, I was grateful I could go to my office, have a life, but secretly I was terrified I'd never work again. Did you know that?

CATHERINE: I wondered.

ROBERT: I was absolutely fucking terrified.

Then I remembered something and a part of the terror went away. I remembered you.

Your creative years were just beginning. You'd get your degree, do your own work. You were just getting started. If you hadn't gone into math, that would have been all right. Claire's done well for herself. I'm satisfied with her.

I'm proud of you.

I don't mean to embarrass you. It's part of the reason we have children. We hope they'll survive us, accomplish what we can't.

Now that I'm back in the game I admit I've got another idea, a better one.

CATHERINE: What?

ROBERT: I know you've got your own work. I don't want you to neglect that. You can't neglect it. But I could probably use some help. Work with me. If you want to, if you can work it out with your class schedule and everything else, I could help you with that, make some calls, talk to your teachers . . .

I'm getting ahead of myself.

Well, Jesus, look, enough bullshit. You asked to see something. Let's start with this. I've roughed something out. General outline for a proof. Major result. Important.

It's not finished but you can see where it's going. Let's see. *(He selects a notebook.)* Here. *(He gives it to* CATHERINE. *She opens it and reads.)* It's very rough.

(After a long moment CATHERINE *closes the notebook. A beat. She sits down next to* ROBERT.*)*

CATHERINE: Dad. Let's go inside.

ROBERT: The gaps might make it hard to follow. We can talk it through.

CATHERINE: You're cold. Let's go in.

ROBERT: Maybe we could work on this together. This might be a great place to start. What about it? What do you think? Let's talk it through.

CATHERINE: Not now. I'm cold too. It's really freezing out here. Let's go inside.

ROBERT: I'm telling you it's stifling in there, goddamn it. The radiators. Look, read out the first couple of lines. That's how we start: you read, and we go line by line, out loud, through the argument. See if there's a better way, a shorter way. Let's collaborate.

CATHERINE: No. Come on.

ROBERT: I've been waiting years for this. This is something I want to do. Come on, let's do some work together.

CATHERINE: We can't do it out here. It's freezing cold. I'm taking you in.

ROBERT: Not until we *talk about the proof.*

CATHERINE: No.

ROBERT: *Goddamnit, Catherine, open the goddamn book and read me the lines.*

(Beat. CATHERINE *opens the book. She reads slowly, without inflection.)*

CATHERINE: "Let X equal the quantity of all quantities of X. Let X equal the cold. It is cold in December. The months of cold equal November through February. There are four months of cold and four of heat, leaving four months of indeterminate temperature. In February it snows. In March the lake is a lake of ice. In September the students come back and the bookstores are full. Let X equal the month of full bookstores. The number of books approaches infinity as the number of months of cold approaches four. I will never be as cold now as I will in the future. The future of cold is infinite. The future of heat is the future of cold. The bookstores are infinite and so are never full except in September . . ." *(She stops reading and slowly closes the book.* ROBERT *is shivering uncontrollably. She puts her arms around him and helps him to his feet.)* It's all right. We'll go inside.

ROBERT: I'm cold.

CATHERINE: We'll warm you up.

ROBERT: Don't leave. Please.

CATHERINE: I won't. Let's go inside.

fade

Scene 5

The present. A week after the events in Scene 3. CLAIRE *on the porch. Coffee in takeout cups.* CLAIRE *takes a plane ticket out of her purse, checks the itinerary. A moment.* CATHERINE *enters with bags for travel.* CLAIRE *gives her a cup of coffee.* CATHERINE *drinks in silence. Beat.*

CATHERINE: Good coffee.

CLAIRE: It's all right, isn't it? *(Beat.)* We have a place where we buy all our coffee. They roast it themselves, they have an old roaster down in the basement. You can smell it on the street. Some mornings you can smell it from our place, four stories up. It's wonderful. "Manhattan's Best": some magazine wrote it up. Who knows. But it is very good.

CATHERINE: Sounds good.

CLAIRE: You'll like it.

CATHERINE: Good.

(Beat.)

CLAIRE: You look nice.

CATHERINE: Thanks, so do you.

(Beat.)

CLAIRE: It's bright.

CATHERINE: Yes.

CLAIRE: It's one of the things I do miss. All the space, the light. You could sit out here all morning.

CATHERINE: It's not that warm.

CLAIRE: Are you cold?

CATHERINE: Not really. I just—

CLAIRE: It has gotten chilly. I'm sorry. Do you want to go in?

CATHERINE: I'm okay.

CLAIRE: I just thought it might be nice to have a quick cup of coffee out here.

CATHERINE: No, it is.

CLAIRE: Plus the kitchen's all put away. If you're cold—

CATHERINE: I'm not. Not really.

CLAIRE: Want your jacket?

CATHERINE: Yeah, okay. (CLAIRE *gives it to her. She puts it on.*) Thanks.

CLAIRE: It's that time of year.

CATHERINE: Yes. You can feel it coming. *(Beat. She stares out at the yard.)*

CLAIRE: Honey, there's no hurry.

CATHERINE: I know.

CLAIRE: If you want to hang out, be alone for a while—

CATHERINE: No. It's no big deal.

CLAIRE: We don't have to leave for twenty minutes or so.

CATHERINE: I know. Thanks, Claire.

CLAIRE: You're all packed.

CATHERINE: Yes.

CLAIRE: If you missed anything it doesn't really matter. The movers will send us everything next month. (CATHERINE *doesn't move. Beat.*) I know this is hard.

CATHERINE: It's fine.

CLAIRE: This is the right decision.

CATHERINE: I know . . .

CLAIRE: I want to do everything I can to make this a smooth transition for you. So does Mitch.

CATHERINE: Good.

CLAIRE: The actual departure is the hardest part. Once we get there we can relax. Enjoy ourselves.

CATHERINE: I know.

(*Beat.*)

CLAIRE: You'll love New York.

CATHERINE: I can't wait.

CLAIRE: You'll love it. It's the most exciting city.

CATHERINE: I know.

CLAIRE: It's not like Chicago, it's really alive.

CATHERINE: I've read about that.

CLAIRE: I think you'll truly feel at home there.

CATHERINE: You know what I'm looking forward to?

CLAIRE: What?

CATHERINE: Seeing Broadway musicals.

(*Beat.*)

CLAIRE: Mitch can get us tickets to whatever you'd like.

CATHERINE: And Rockefeller Center in winter—all the skaters!

CLAIRE: Well, you—

CATHERINE: Also, the many fine museums!

(*Beat.*)

CLAIRE: I know how hard this is for you.

CATHERINE: Listening to you say how hard it is for me is what's hard for me.

CLAIRE: Once you're there you'll see all the possibilities that are available.

CATHERINE: Restraints, lithium, electroshock.

CLAIRE: *Schools.* In the New York area alone there's NYU, Columbia—

CATHERINE: Bright college days! Football games, road trips, necking on the "quad."

CLAIRE: Or if that's not what you want we can help you find a job. Mitch has terrific contacts all over town.

CATHERINE: Does he know anyone in the phone-sex industry?

CLAIRE: I want to make this as easy a transition as I can.

CATHERINE: It's going to be *easy*, Claire, it's gonna be so fucking easy you won't believe it.

CLAIRE: Thank you.

CATHERINE: I'm going to sit quietly on the plane to New York. And live quietly in a cute apartment. And answer Dr. Von Heimlich's questions very politely.

CLAIRE: You can see any doctor you like, or you can see no doctor.

CATHERINE: I would like to see a doctor called Dr. Von Heimlich: please find one. And I would like him to wear a monocle. And I'd like him to have a very soft, very well-upholstered couch, so that I'll be perfectly comfortable while I'm blaming everything on you.

(Beat.)

CLAIRE: Don't come.

CATHERINE: No, I'm coming.

CLAIRE: Stay here, see how you do.

CATHERINE: I could.

CLAIRE: You can't take care of yourself for *five days*.

CATHERINE: Bullshit!

CLAIRE: You *slept all week*. I had to cancel my flight. I missed a week of work— I was this close to taking you to the hospital! I couldn't believe it when you finally dragged yourself up.

CATHERINE: I was tired!

CLAIRE: You were completely out of it, Catherine, you weren't speaking!

CATHERINE: I didn't want to talk to you.

(Beat.)

CLAIRE: Stay here if you hate me so much.

CATHERINE: And do what?

CLAIRE: You're the genius, figure it out.

(CLAIRE is upset, near tears. She digs in her bag, pulls out a plane ticket, throws it on the table. She exits. CATHERINE is alone. She can't quite bring herself to leave the porch. A moment. HAL enters—not through the house, from the side. He is badly dressed and looks very tired. He is breathless from running.)

HAL: You're still here. *(CATHERINE is surprised. She doesn't speak.)* I saw Claire leaving out front. I wasn't sure if you— *(He holds up the notebook.)* This fucking thing . . . checks out.

I have been over it, *twice*, with two different sets of guys, old geeks *and* young geeks. It is *weird*. I don't know where the techniques came from. Some of the moves are very hard to follow. But we can't find anything wrong with it! There might be something wrong with it but we can't find it. I have not slept. *(He catches his breath.)* It works. I thought you might want to know.

CATHERINE: I already knew.

(Beat.)

HAL: I had to swear these guys to secrecy. They were jumping out of their skins. See, one e-mail and it's all over. I threatened them. I think we're safe, they're physical cowards. *(Beat.)* I had to see you.

CATHERINE: I'm leaving.

HAL: I know. Just wait for a minute, please?

CATHERINE: What do you want? You have the book. She told

me you came by for it and she gave it to you. You can do whatever you want with it. Publish it.

HAL: Catherine.

CATHERINE: Get Claire's permission and publish it. She doesn't care. She doesn't know anything about it anyway.

HAL: I don't want Claire's permission.

CATHERINE: You want mine? Publish. Go for it. Have a press conference. Tell the world what my father discovered.

HAL: I don't want to.

CATHERINE: Or fuck my father, pass it off as your own work. Who cares? Write your own ticket to any math department in the country.

HAL: I don't think your father wrote it.

(Beat.)

CATHERINE: You thought so last week.

HAL: That was last week. I spent this week reading the proof. I think I understand it, more or less. It uses a lot of newer mathematical techniques, things that were developed in the last decade. Elliptic curves. Modular forms. I think I learned more mathematics this week than I did in four years of grad school.

CATHERINE: So?

HAL: So the proof is very . . . hip.

CATHERINE: Get some sleep, Hal.

HAL: What was your father doing the last ten years? He wasn't well, was he?

CATHERINE: Are you done?

HAL: I don't think he would have been able to master those new techniques.

CATHERINE: But he was a genius.

HAL: But he was nuts.

CATHERINE: So he read about them later.

HAL: Maybe. The books he would have needed are upstairs.
(Beat.)

79

Your dad dated everything. Even his most incoherent entries he dated. There are no dates in this.

CATHERINE: The handwriting—

HAL: —looks like your dad's. Parents and children sometimes have similar handwriting, especially if they've spent a lot of time together.

(Beat.)

CATHERINE: Interesting theory.

HAL: I like it.

CATHERINE: I like it too. It's what I told you last week.

HAL: I know.

CATHERINE: You blew it.

HAL: I—

CATHERINE: It's too bad, the rest of it was really good. All of it: "I loved your dad." "I always liked you." "I'd like to spend every minute with you . . ." It's killer stuff. You got laid *and* you got the notebook! You're a genius!

HAL: You're giving me way too much credit. (*Beat.*) I don't expect you to be happy with me. I just wanted . . . I don't know. I was hoping to discuss some of this with you before you left. Purely professional. I don't expect anything else.

CATHERINE: Forget it.

HAL: I mean we have questions. Working on this must have been amazing. I'd love just to hear you talk about some of it.

CATHERINE: No.

HAL: You'll have to deal with it eventually, you know. You can't ignore it, you'll have to get it published. You'll have to talk to someone.

Take it, at least. Then I'll go. Here.

CATHERINE: I don't want it.

HAL: Come on, Catherine. I'm trying to correct things.

CATHERINE: You *can't*. Do you hear me?

You think you've figured something out? You run over

here so pleased with yourself because you changed your mind. Now you're certain. You're so . . . *sloppy*. You don't know anything. The book, the math, the dates, the writing, all that stuff you decided with your buddies, it's just evidence. It doesn't finish the job. It doesn't prove anything.

HAL: Okay, what would?

CATHERINE: *Nothing.*

You should have trusted me.

(Beat.)

HAL: I know. *(Beat.* CATHERINE *gathers her things.)* So Claire sold the house?

CATHERINE: Yes.

HAL: Stay in Chicago. You're an adult.

CATHERINE: She wants me in New York. She wants to look after me.

HAL: Do you need looking after?

CATHERINE: She thinks I do.

HAL: You looked after your dad for five years.

CATHERINE: So maybe it's my turn.

I kick and scream, but I don't know. Being taken care of, it doesn't sound so bad. I'm tired.

And the house is a wreck, let's face it. It was my dad's house . . .

(Beat.)

HAL: Nice house.

CATHERINE: It's old.

HAL: I guess.

CATHERINE: It's drafty as hell. The winters are rough.

HAL: That's just Chicago.

CATHERINE: Either it's freezing inside, or the steam's on full-blast and you're stifling.

HAL: I don't mind cold weather. Keeps you alert.

CATHERINE: Wait a few years.

HAL: I've lived here all my life.

CATHERINE: Yeah?

HAL: Sure. Just like you.

CATHERINE: Still. I don't think I should spend another winter here.

(Beat.)

HAL: There is nothing wrong with you.

CATHERINE: I think I'm like my dad.

HAL: I think you are too.

CATHERINE: I'm . . . *afraid* I'm like my dad.

HAL: You're not him.

CATHERINE: Maybe I will be.

HAL: Maybe. Maybe you'll be better.

(Pause. HAL *hands her the book. This time* CATHERINE *takes it. She sits. She looks down at the book, runs her fingers over the cover.)*

CATHERINE: It didn't feel "amazing" or—what word did you use?

HAL: Yeah, amazing.

CATHERINE: Yeah. It was just connecting the dots.

Some nights I could connect three or four. Some nights they'd be really far apart, I'd have no idea how to get to the next one, if there was a next one.

HAL: He really never knew?

CATHERINE: No. I worked after midnight. He was usually in bed.

HAL: Every night?

CATHERINE: No. When I got stuck I watched TV. Sometimes if he couldn't sleep he'd come downstairs, sit with me. We'd talk. Not about math, he couldn't. About the movie we were watching. I'd explain the stories.

Or about fixing the heat. Decide we didn't want to. We liked the radiators even though they clanked in the middle of the night, made the air dry.

Or we'd plan breakfast, talk about what we were gonna eat together in the morning.

Those nights were usually pretty good.

I know . . . it works . . . But all I can see are the compromises, the approximations, places where it's stitched together. It's lumpy. Dad's stuff was way more elegant. When he was young.

(Beat.)

HAL: Talk me through it? Whatever's bothering you. Maybe you'll improve it.

CATHERINE: I don't know . . .

HAL: Pick anything. Give it a shot? Maybe you'll discover something elegant.

(A moment. HAL sits next to CATHERINE. Eventually she opens the book, turns the pages slowly, finding a section. She looks at him.)

CATHERINE: Here.

(She begins to speak.)

curtain